Empowering Students to Transform Schools

"Students are the primary focus of everything we do as educators. That's why giving students a voice as we make decisions is so very important. Not only will they provide insights into making schools even more effective, they will also learn how a truly democratic institution involves those it serves. **Empowering Students to Transform Schools** will surely provide valuable advice for consideration by everyone who cares about kids and our collective future."

  —**Gary Marx,** *Senior Associate Executive Director,*
  American Association of School Administrators

"Building a learner-centered school has for the most part been evolving without any direction. This book, **Empowering Students to Transform Schools** by Gary Goldman and Jay Newman, provides a well thought-out plan for developing learner-centered schools. We have known for a long time that those who are affected by change need to be active participants in the process. Goldman and Newman have captured in their book the steps needed to truly reconceptualize our educational system!"

  —**Phillip Harris,** *Director, Professional Development, Phi Delta Kappa*

"The authors have tapped into the power of viewing students as colleagues, rather than as customers or products. Allowing students the opportunity to take ownership of their education from kindergarten on will ensure that they become learners for life."

  —**David P. Langford,** *President, Langford International, Inc., Montana*

"*Sling Blade* is a kindred spirit to this book in that both are deeply committed to the idea of enriching life's textures and promoting strong character development of disadvantaged children. Educators will find adopting this unique program an inspirational and vital resource. We need more investment from students in their own destiny where they develop increased responsibility and respect. Read this book—it has great heart."

  —**Billy Bob Thornton,** *Academy Award winning writer, and*
  best actor nominee, **Sling Blade**

"Those things which children cherish become those things which they feel responsibility toward. Goldman and Newman explore some of the most interesting ways in which real responsibility for schools can be shared with students. The results of their techniques are spectacular."

  —**John Abbott,** *Director of Education 2000, President of 21st Century*
  Learning Initiative, Washington, DC

"This books steps back from just looking at philosophical issues and offers the opportunity to understand real life situations, with real people making real change."

  —**Patricia Wightman,** *Asst. Director, Michigan Quality Council*

"I highly recommend this book for any educator who wants to build a positive school climate and successful learning environment. Students need to be empowered to take responsibility for positive change and to become successful contributors in all areas of society. This is exactly what this practical book and its innovative leadership program does–gives our young people a role to play in improving our nation's education system."

  —**Edgar Lopez,** *State Representative 4th District, Illinois, Vice-Chair,*
  Education Appropriations Committee

"**Empowering Students to Transform Schools** is an important tool for all involved in the educational process so that students are given the power they need to change their schools for the better."

—**Ben Smilowitz,** *Chair and Co-Founder, International Student Activism Alliance, CT*

"The authors have given us a precious gift, a framework for our children to be able to contribute to us, the adults, in the healing of our schools and communities."

—**Steven Vannoy,** *author,* **The 10 Greatest Gifts I Give My Children and The Greatest Gifts Our Children Give to Us**

"This book's focus on student leadership and empowerment is critical. We must begin to view students as the subject and not as the objects of education. This book provides the tools for students to positively challenge the power relationships that often strangle public education."

—**Paul Schmitz,** *Vice President and Chief Strategist, Public Allies, Washington, DC*

"The authors speak to the urgent need to prepare students for the future with the skills of leadership, self-esteem, compassion, problem-solving, and teamwork. This very timely book helps to realize this vision in very powerful and human ways. It is a landmark work that is destined to contribute powerfully to dynamic breakthroughs in our schools."

—**Margaret Evans,** *Assistant Executive Director for Student Services, National Association for Elementary School Principals*

"Through nearly thirty years of teaching and coaching, I have longed for a solid, practical way to empower students with the skills and abilities needed to become constructive change agents within their educational setting. This book and its dynamic process of 'Quality Student Leadership' has definitely been a positive and productive answer. It gives the step-by-step methodology than enables them to be agents of change, not only now, but for the future. It helps the entire school community, regardless of differences, to focus and plan, together for personal, group, and systems change and growth."

—**Don Logan,** *Counselor, Benton Community High School, Iowa, Executive Secretary of the Iowa Basketball Coaches Assoc.*

"Your book is an excellent blueprint for educational organizations to develop plans for full participation from parents, school staff, community and students. I especially enjoyed 'Making Commitments', 'Creating the Vision', and 'Building a Schoolwide Culture for Self-Esteem.' They provide an excellent plan for empowering those who deal with the at-risk population and all its stakeholders."

—**Barbara V. Williams,** *Center for School Improvement, University of Chicago*

"This lively and readable book is written by two progressive educators who approach the issue of transforming schools in progressive, imaginative, and constructive ways without at any time preaching to schools and teachers. It is a welcome–and exciting–refocusing on what really matters in education, the success of students."

—**John Rennie,** *Founding Director, CEDC, United Kingdom*

"We share your belief that until a student is fully engaged in the process and committed to the goal, we have little chance of being as successful as we need in preparing students for the 21st century. We support your vision of creating alliances with others who have similar goals and expertise, where these ideas can be distributed into every school and every neighborhood the nation. This book is a call to action now."

—**Dan Bassill,** *President and Chief Executive Officer,*
Tutor/Mentor Connection

"At last–a book that gives a real recognition to the central role of students in shaping school outcomes and in determining the real impact of reform in schools. Every educator in school reform should read this book!"

—**Benjamin Levin,** *Dean, Continuing Education, University of Manitoba,*
Winnipeg, Canada

"This is a book not only of dynamic principles that are vital to shaping our children's future, but it is a book with heart. This is an important book for counselors, psychologists, social workers, gifted and special education professionals, and any educator who is interested in learning about a practical and straightforward approach to engaging our students in their own education."

—**Charlene Vega,** *Pupil Support Services Officer, Chicago Public Schools*

"Our greatest renewable resource is our children. If we do not equip them with the best education then we will impair our nation's ability to complete globally. A key component to make this happen is to get students involved in and responsible for their own education. The authors show us how to do this on a local, regional, and national basis. This is the kind of thinking and specific action steps we need to improve the quality of our education and empower our youth to lead us into the future."

—**Gregory C. Vrablik,** *Executive Director, Presidents Forum*

"I find myself in deep accord with your long-term objectives. Change must come from the students themselves if it is to be at all meaningful. And if we want to teach them to be vital citizens in an actualized democracy we must first empower them to direct needed changes in their school environment."

—**Frederick Marx,** *Producer,* **Hoop Dreams**

"I wholeheartedly endorse this book and its philosophy that all children can learn, be viewed as valued members of the school, and develop those proactive leadership skills that can contribute to transforming a school community. Every principal across America can benefit from reading this dynamic book."

—**Audrey Donaldson,** *Principal, Gage Park High School,*
Chicago Public Schools

"The authors have laid out a clear blueprint for student participation in improving education."

—**John Roger,** *Institute for Individual and World Peace;*
Chancellor, University of Santa Monica, California

Empowering Students to Transform Schools

Gary Goldman
Jay B. Newman

CORWIN PRESS, INC.
A Sage Publications Company
Thousand Oaks, California

For information:

Corwin Press, Inc.
A Sage Publications Company
2455 Teller Road
Thousand Oaks, California 91320
E-mail: order@corwin.sagepub.com

SAGE Publications Ltd.
6 Bonhill Street
London EC2A 4PU
United Kingdom

SAGE Publications India Pvt. Ltd.
M-32 Market
Greater Kailash I
New Delhi 110 048 India

Printed in the United States of America

Library of Congress Cataloging-in-Publication Data

Goldman, Gary, 1951–
    Empowering students to transform schools / by Gary Goldman and Jay B. Newman.
        p. cm.
    Includes bibliographical references.
    ISBN 0-8039-6547-8 (cloth: acid-free paper). — ISBN
0-8039-6548-6 (pbk.: acid-free paper)
    1. School improvement programs—United States. 2. Student
participation in administration—United States. 3. Educational
leadership—United States. 4. School environment—United States.
5. Students—United States—Attitudes. I. Newman, Jay B.
II. Title.
LB2822.82.G65 1998
371.8—dc21   97-33825

This book is printed on acid-free paper.

98 99 00 01 02 03 10 9 8 7 6 5 4 3 2 1

Production Editor: Astrid Virding
Production Assistant: Karen Wiley
Corwin Editorial Assistant: Kristen L. Gibson
Typesetter/Designer: Christina M. Hill
Cover Designer: Marcia M. Rosenburg
Print Buyer: Anna Chin

Contents

Preface

This book has been written to address the needs of school administrators, teachers, and counselors. This book is about the empowerment of students to transform schools. The school professionals hold the key to opening up schools and allowing parents, community members, and students to fully participate in the processes of quality education. Therefore, it is our intent to capture the imagination and spirit of those dedicated professional who have the opportunity to shape the schools of the 21st century.

There are numerous books on a variety of means for improving the quality of schools. We are not aware, however, of any books that directly address the importance of student involvement in the process. What if we empowered students as partners in change and took the risk to work with them in dynamic new ways? Is it possible that the adults in some schools have become too rigid and secure in our "knowing what is best" and that a fresh point-of-view offered by students might open new doors for improvement? This is a book of revelation. It reveals the power of our youth. They are ready, willing, and able to help communities transform schools into true learning communities. Some students have already been invited to assist in changing their schools from institutions into dynamic, living organisms; schools with a heart.

As worldwide education is examined, it appears that every community is looking for innovative programs and strategies that will improve the quality of schools. Most existing models have one common thread; they focus on how we are going to increase student achievement on national and international standardized tests. Although we acknowledge the importance of this focus, in our experience, there needs to be an emphasis on the whole child. First and foremost, we do not believe that education is about doing something to students. It is our belief that education is about students assimilating their personal experiences into a repertoire of knowledge, skills, and behaviors that will allow them to successfully relate to the world. To accomplish this requires that schools focus on the root of education, "educo" which means to lead out from *within* a student's own innate wisdom.

Lost in today's push for academic excellence is the vital importance of seemingly "unmeasurable skills." Love, friendship, integrity, compassion, faith, hope—these are but a few of the many intangibles that determine the quality of our society yet cannot be directly measured. Therefore, they are often left out of the education equation. It is part of the dynamic vision of this book to demonstrate how schools and communities can incorporate these skills into learning environments. It is necessary to find a means for measuring this impact of education. In light of the number of young people who drop out of school, drop into gangs, tune out of society, and tune into drugs, it becomes our role as educators to create school experiences that invite the disenfranchised students back into a productive role in society. When given the proper environment for learning and growing, students can discover their real value and place in the world. Throughout this book, stories and experiences of young people, from kindergarten to high school, are offered as examples of student empowerment and involvement. Through an expanded style of teaching and learning, students open up and find that they are capable of great success.

It is our sincere belief that all children can learn. We do not believe that all children come to the table with the same appetite and the same tastes, but it is the role of society to make certain that all children are fed. This book demonstrates how bringing students of all achievement levels together in empowering activities makes for a rich synergizing experience. As diverse students interact, the strengths of each are maximized, and the weaknesses are strengthened. To separate and isolate denies the "weaker" students the opportunity to show their strengths and prevents the "stronger" students from having enriching experiences that challenge their abilities to work in a diverse community. No matter what students' status might be, they all deserve to be viewed as valued members of a school community where mutual support and trust are built.

The vision and mission with which this book was written can be seen through the progression of ideas in each chapter. Chapter 1, "Developing Excellence Through Student Leadership," begins the journey by demonstrating how student involvement can be used to alter the culture of a school. Examples of specific projects and processes are used to show how schools can take charge of their own transformation. Chapter 2, "Making Commitments and Sharing the Vision," focuses on the importance of committing to a vision. Many schools have the goal to utilize students to help achieve excellence. However, without a significant commitment to a common vision of what excellence looks like, the chances of achieving the goal will be diminished. Chapter 3, "Building a Schoolwide Culture for Self-Esteem," recognizes that how students feel about themselves and their school is directly related to how much they participate in the processes of school.

Beginning in Chapter 4, "Teambuilding and Organization With Students," the book shifts into a discussion of strategies that have been used to increase student involvement and empowerment. Specifically, Chapter 4 provides some examples of the types of teams that can be formed to assist in the inclusion of students in the processes of school. It also provides some insight into how schools help these teams be more productive. Being focused on action is at the core of this book. Chapter 5, "Generating Creative Success: Planning for Action," takes the concept of the team forward toward the development of specific plans for achieving desired outcomes. Problem identification, problem-solving, decision making, and action-planning techniques and strategies are provided as examples of what schools might do. The key of this chapter, however, is the realization that each strategy must be molded to the needs of an individual school and its unique circumstances. Chapter 6, "Evaluating Progress," discussed strategies and techniques for measuring progress toward goals. A case is made for having students participate in this aspect of a school's continuous quality improvement efforts. The final chapter, Chapter 7, "Student Leadership in Future Learning Communities," explains where we hope schools will be in the future. By empowering students to transform schools, it is our hope that a vision of learning organizations can be realized. Furthermore, it is hoped that, in the not-too-distant future, schools will take on the role of facilitator of learning for the entire community.

We have included additional resources to help support the student empowerment process. Resource A includes charts, surveys, and worksheets to be used in the implementation of your student empowerment program. Resource B has an example of a Quality Student Leadership Assessment. Resource C contains the Sturgis High School "Sense of Belonging" Student Survey.

At the very conclusion of the book is our "Empowering Students to Transform Schools Project." It is our intention, through our International Quality Leadership Institute, to mobilize our youth worldwide by providing training and involvement in projects and networks for positive global experiences and the betterment of humankind. We invite you to form an alliance with us to support this vision for our students, and all the children of the world.

—Gary Goldman
Chicago, Illinois

—Jay B. Newman
Sturgis, Michigan

Acknowledgments

For all of those along the way who kept believing with us that our children are our most precious asset . . . and who put themselves on the line to demonstrate their belief. It is with utmost gratitude that we name but a few.

My father and mother, David and Anna Goldman; my sisters, Diana, Linda, and Janice; to my dedicated colleagues, Ron Mark and Irwin Aloff; to the many teachers who have inspired my work; special thanks to the educators who have supported my vision, Jack Canfield, Robert Goodwin, Lynn St. James, Jean Houston, David Langford, Gary Marx, Philip Harris, Sara Lynch, Audrey Donaldson, Virginia Vaske, Jose Rodriguez, Alice Peters, Joseph Spagnolo, David Turner, John Rennie, Joe Herrity, George Pintar, Don Logan, Ray Morley, Mary Maly, Paul Messier, Candy Cash, Ed Klunk, Roosevelt Burnett, Jean Baxter, Larry Freeman, Cheryl Cholar, Margaret Byrnes, Ed Wolf, John Simmons, Allen Smith, Robert Saddler, Harriet O'Donnell, Dennis Williams, Bertha Murray, Jacqueline Simmons, Lois Gilmore, Gretchen Alexander, and Kay Brown; to those who supported my corporate education partnerships, Dean Mefford, Gerry Roper, and Bill Tuggle; to Alice Foster and the Corwin Press staff for their professional expertise; in appreciation to my coauthor and fellow educator, Jay Newman; and to all of the students who have continually inspired me.

—Gary Goldman

For my wife, Barbara; my children, Matt, Pete, and Kari; my mother, JoAnn Newman; my mother-in-law, Marilyn Joynt; my grandmother, Bertie Shobe; my brothers, Mark and Bert; and in memory of my sister, Alison, my father, Albert H. Newman Jr., and my father-in-law, John J. Joynt. With thanks to the more than 10,000 students with whom I have the opportunity to work and who have taught me well, but especially the following students, who showed me how to lead: Andrew Parial, Patty Cronley, Mike Roberts, Tom Cronley, Kristin Allen, Amber Picker, Doris Burghduff, Rhonda Metz, Kaery O'Dell, Keith Mack, and Vincent Cabansag. Special thanks to the hundreds of teachers and administrators who have influenced my career, and my heartfelt gratitude to my mentors: Bill Furtwengler; Don Lueder; Kent Peterson; Vi Schuler; Wendell Moyer; Skip Sisson; Larry Hubley; Lowell (Wally) Walsworth; Kent Roberts; and my colleague, associate, coauthor, and friend, Gary Goldman.

—Jay B. Newman

Quality Student Learning—Planning and Development support by Randy Bennett, Chicago, IL.

Graphics: Paco Aramburu and Anita Fontana (In Your Own Image) Chicago, IL.

For those we have not named, know that we carry you all in our hearts.

—Gary and Jay

About the Authors

Gary Goldman, a recognized leader in education reform, has a unique gift for reaching and inspiring the hearts, minds, and spirit of our young people. As a champion of students, he has dedicated himself to the development of quality schools that involve students as positive change agents. His model supports students and adults, working as active participants and partners, in the creation of learning communities. The process provides a framework for creating positive learning environments that prepare students with the academic, social, and leadership skills necessary for the 21st century.

Mr. Goldman consults with elementary and secondary schools in urban and rural settings as a trainer and facilitator of innovative programs that meet the needs of students, teachers, administrators, parents, and community members. His K-12 curriculum educates adults and students in total quality education, transformational learning and leadership, and empowerment for school and community application. Colleges are incorporating this text and his workbooks into their syllabus. Published works include the comprehensive *Qual-*

ity Leadership Workbook, Quality Student Leadership Workbook and Facilitator Guide, Quality Student Learning Guide, and his current book, *Empowering Students to Transform Schools.*

Gary Goldman is acclaimed as a dynamic and knowledgeable speaker for a wide-range of multicultural audiences. His presentations to school communities have proven invaluable in applying practical strategies in their organizations. He is a guest lecturer at universities and presents at national conferences. He has traveled to England to present his American model to British educators.

Mr. Goldman's innovative school improvement programs have received recognition in the media, including ABC, The Learning Channel, and Tokyo Broadcasting System, and radio and newspapers. He has hosted a weekly Chicago radio show on education called "Champions of Our Children."

Gary Goldman holds a M.A. in organizational development and is president and founder of Quality Improvement Associates, Inc. (QIA). QIA is an international consulting firm serving school districts, communities, and corporations in the development of educational models, and quality leadership and human resource projects. As a result of his extensive pioneering efforts and vision, Mr. Goldman has created the non-profit International Quality Leadership Institute dedicated to empowering students and adults to work collaboratively for school, community, and global transformation.

Jay B. Newman has been leaving his mark on education for the past 25 years. Initially, he was a classroom science teacher and coach, but over the past 15 years, he has been an administrator, lecturer, and workshop presenter. A constant desire to get students, parents, and community more involved in what goes on in school led Dr. Newman to the creation of a broad-based coalition of stakeholders in the school and community improvement process. As a result of this work, he has been sought after to help other schools increase student, parent, and community involvement. His program has been recognized in the book *Quality Education,* by Gray Rinehart; in the Eye on Education's 1993 publication *Innovations in Education;* and in the Learning Channel's TeacherTV program, which focused on the "Changing Role of Students" (aired in the fall of 1995 and again in the spring of 1996). Sturgis High School, where his program has been implemented, will soon be one of 50 high schools to be featured in a book being written by Paul S. George and Ken McEwin titled *The Exemplary High School*. Dr. Newman is also the author of several articles.

Currently, Dr. Newman is Assistant Superintendent of the Sturgis Public Schools, Michigan. Prior to this position, he served 2 years as high school principal and as assistant principal for the previous 4 years. It was as the assistant principal that Dr. Newman brought these exciting programs to Sturgis High School. As the principal, he had the opportunity to receive many accolades for his work, and now, as the assistant superintendent, he can bring the principles of quality to the entire district. As a presenter, Dr. Newman brings excitement and enthusiasm to his audiences. His mixture of humor and research-based information leaves workshop attendees wanting to continue the experience. The practical nature of his message has immediate applicability for teachers and students alike.

1

Developing Excellence Through Student Leadership

Each of us must do our part, no matter where we live, in city or countryside. Children are quick to see the value of individual action. All around the world, when I talk to them, I find them aware . . . and convinced they can make a difference, and eager to help. Therein, lies our hope . . . more and more people are opening their hearts to the desperation they see around them and springing into action. For this is how we can attain our human potential for compassion and for love.

—Jane Goodall (*National Geographic*)

The quality of any school is generally defined by the quality of work produced and the quality of behaviors displayed by the students in that school. Schools have consistently adopted programs that staff and administration believe will increase learning, improve test scores, reduce inappropriate and unacceptable behaviors, and decrease absenteeism. All too often, schools have forgotten input from the most critical stakeholders in the process of education: the students.

For the past 12 years, we have been working with students at many different levels in both public and private schools. The goal has been to help them become part of a national drive toward the continuous improvement of education, and to help schools attain the level of excellence that they desire and the nation now demands. There is great reason to be optimistic and to believe that the goal is within sight. The nation has established Goals 2000, and every state has made the improvement of its schools a top priority. How schools within each state meet these expectations has been left up to them, and this has left many school authorities searching for the formula that works.

An important piece to the puzzle has been found. It may not be the whole puzzle, but schools using the plans that will be discussed in this book have experienced dramatic improvements. Much of the literature on continuous improvement of schools and other organizations emphasizes the importance of stakeholder involvement. It has been observed that involving students in the transformation of a school significantly improves the culture of that school. In most cases, continuous improvement will become the focus of the school culture within a few years. (See Figure 1.1.)

The key factor is meaningful student involvement, as opposed to the all-too-frequent token involvement. A classic example of token student involvement was the case of the Chicago public schools and the mandate that students be included in the Local School Councils (LSCs) established through school improvement legislation. Initially, these students were selected to represent the students from the high school governed by the LSC. There were 75 such councils throughout the city of Chicago. Therefore, there were 75 student representatives selected to help create a more positive educational culture in the Chicago public schools. There was one major catch to this setup. None of the students had a vote on any of these LSCs. Therefore, very few of the adults paid much attention to these "kids."

The student LSC representatives got together and asked Gary Goldman to help them get organized into a cohesive group. Their hope was that they might be able to demonstrate to city leaders, school district leaders, and state legislators that they had the knowledge, skills, and abilities necessary to be taken seriously and given a voice on these councils. As a result of the Quality Student Leadership training these students received, several students formed committees that had specific tasks to accomplish. Those committees' goals ranged from curriculum to safety to lobbying the state legislature for the right to vote at LSC meetings. As a result of their work, changes occurred. Most notable of these was that the student representatives earned the right to vote on the LSCs.

The events of the Chicago experience set the pace for a journey that has been both exciting and, at times, frustrating. The old paradigm that children are to be seen but not heard continues to be a major mode of operation in many school districts. This is the case in spite of many successes and research data that show that schools that empower

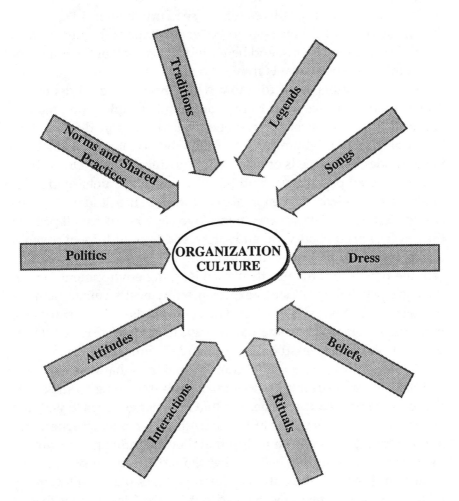

Together, these factors influence the long-term success and day-to-day performance of the entire organization and every person associated with it more powerfully than any formal control system could possibly do.

Figure 1.1. Organization culture is everything that influences how stakeholders think, feel, and behave.

students have a more positive culture (see Furtwengler, 1991, p. 72). This positive culture translates to better attendance, higher grades, fewer discipline problems, and better test scores—all of the improvements that everybody wants from schools.

Many educators want to know why empowering students improves schools. The answer to this question is simple. The practical application of this concept, however, can be a little more difficult than its simple nature might imply. The foundation of empowerment lies in the fundamental needs of all people. The influences of Dr. William Glasser—noted psychiatrist, author, and, as of late, trainer in ideas of quality schools—can be seen in many of the Quality Student Leadership materials. Dr. Glasser recognizes five basic needs for all people: the physical need of survival and safety, and four additional psychological needs of fun, power, freedom, and belonging. When students lack the power to influence their own learning environment, one of the basic psychological needs experienced by every human being is not being met. When schools do not meet the needs of their customers, those customers will find alternative ways to meet those needs. Thus, the class clown, the classroom lawyer, and the bully are born.

Another blockade to school transformation is that many schools still believe that learning has to be painful if it is going to stick. It is almost as if some educators believe that knowledge seeps in with the emotional wounds that they inflict. In truth, all too often, teachers and administrators do not even realize that they are inflicting the wound they inflict. They simply believe that the old paradigm of "learn or we'll punish you" is the only way learning takes place. Today, many educators are finding, as is pointed out by Dr. Glasser, that fear of punishment yields minimal compliance and does not produce excellence. If society wants students to succeed and demonstrate excellence, steps must be taken to make sure that they want to be in school and that learning is satisfying. When students are empowered, they have the opportunity to affect their school culture. They have a chance to influence the climate in a way that can make learning more satisfying.

A common fear, voiced by many educators, is that once empowered, students will want to make changes in schools that will not be in the best interests of students in general. There is also a concern that once students are given the power to affect changes in the school, the adult authorities will lose control of the school. The truth is that schools that are run as benevolent dictatorships truly do not have the students under their control. Students may comply minimally with the directives of the dictatorship, but they will not produce the level of quality improvements that schools really need. In addition, as soon as the authoritative back is turned, the students will take advantage of every loophole and security breach they possibly can. True control results when students and staff both conduct themselves in a manner that is best for all people in the culture.

Does empowering students really make a difference? One high school that has used the Quality Student Leadership (QSL) model has seen the type of results that most schools are urgently seeking. Sturgis High School, in Sturgis, Michigan, has been using QSL for the past 6 years and has seen some radical improvements in the school culture. Sturgis is a rural community approximately 45 miles east of South Bend, Indiana. The high school has 850 9th- through 12th-grade students and has a long tradition of excellence. Many people might say things are good, and don't fix what isn't broken. But the administration at Sturgis High School said, "If we're not getting better, we must be losing ground. Sometimes, what appears to be whole and unbroken are tools that fit machines which are no longer in use. Therefore, let's see what we can do to make things better."

In the spring of 1991, QSL was introduced to the students and faculty at Sturgis High School. A core of 40 student leaders attended a one-half-day workshop in preparation for learning about QSL. That workshop was conducted by Dr. Jay Newman, Assistant Principal at that time, and Mr. Lyle Sisson, Assistant Superintendent. The purpose of this initial workshop was to let these students know why we were getting involved in the process of school improvement and why we intended to have students participate in the process. One month later, these same students were introduced to Gary Goldman, who taught them the concepts of QSL.

During the QSL workshop, students learned to envision a new concept of school based on a new philosophy and a new paradigm of school. As a result of that workshop, a new vision and direction was created. In the afternoon of this day, the 40 students were combined with staff members to work on task teams that would focus on school improvement goals. Before these teams began their work, the students reported out on their hopes and dreams for the future of Sturgis High School. When their vision was shared, the staff responded with, "When do we get to share our hopes and dreams with the students?" Now was definitely the time. What they found was that students and teachers wanted essentially the same things.

At this point, faculty and students, along with parents and community members, embarked on a journey that was aimed at making significant improvements in our school. Five critical areas were identified that both students and faculty believed would help to improve our school. First and foremost was the desire to help students feel as if they belonged at Sturgis High School. This team became our Sense of Belonging team. The other four teams focused on goals of improving critical and creative thinking skills, tolerance for diversity, the improvement of informational reading skills, and increasing personal responsibility. Students have come and gone over these past 6 years, but students continue to work on these teams, and, along with faculty, parents, and community members, the efforts are still made to make Sturgis High School a better place.

The events at Sturgis High School have been significant. The product of the work done will provide important evidence as to the effectiveness of our programs. Therefore, it will be relevant to revisit this school and its progress throughout various sections of this book.

What Student Leadership Can Do for the School

The QSL process provides a vehicle for helping students, as well as teachers and parents, become full and active partners in their schools and communities. Experience confirms that people will not commit or even care about institutions to which they do not belong. Conversely, people will commit and work hard for a school and community to which they do belong. The number-one cause of disruptive behavior in most high schools is a pervasive feeling of disconnectedness. There are large numbers of parents who are not involved in their school community. There are large numbers of students who drop out of school, and many of these feel they do not belong. Research indicates that there is a high correlation between students who feel that "nobody cares about me" and students who drop out. The best education is one in which parents and students buy in and feel, "I am part of this school."

The QSL process trains students to take more ownership in their schools and communities and become active partners in school and community improvement. Research shows that students who are directly involved have an increase in their sense of responsibility for the organization. Students can contribute significantly to improving their schools. A powerful payoff for this involvement is not only more improvement for schools and communities, but also new behaviors that contribute to a positive culture are reinforced. In other words, students who have ownership in their organization tend to take personal responsibility for their education (Furtwengler, 1990). We believe that teachers need to be trained in a new paradigm of teaching and learning in the classroom. When there is a true relationship built between students and adults, intrinsic motivation is enhanced. When teachers are facilitators of learning, not information givers, and leaders, not bosses, in the classroom, risk-taking, change, and transformation are the norm.

The QSL process builds partnerships and learning communities between students, teachers, parents, employers, and community—all working together to assist in a cultural shift. People begin to see themselves and the organization in new ways that support their, and the organization's, uniqueness. The process is community and student centered; and because it is a process, there will be ongoing change with challenges to face. The key is adaptability and continual course correction for improvements.

Schools, even the low-achieving ones, can change positively and dramatically as they create a community in which the goal is not to do something to students but for students to become productive workers and leaders. When such a cultural change is undertaken, the school becomes a significant force in moving the community to higher levels of decency and humanity. The bottom line is that communities need to create schools of excellence. Society cannot abandon its youth. The school must become an extended family. Schools need to take a more extensive role in the lives of youth and become a safe haven in which children can grow and become contributors to society.

So, how do schools get young people to grow into contributors to society and learn how to lead? The focus of the entire QSL process is the development of personal skills that will allow students to be leaders. One of our most recently developed strategies is the 10 Characteristics of Quality Student Leaders.

---

10 Characteristics of Quality Student Leaders

L	Learning
E	Empathy
A	Attitude
D	Dedication
E	Energy
R	Respect
S	Service
H	Honesty
I	Ingenuity
P	Passion

Learning is essential for the Quality Student Leader. In every situation and circumstance, there is some knowledge, skill, or ability that can be acquired. Whether it is how to complete a task or how certain people respond to stresses in their environment, the Quality Student Leader shows an understanding of the importance of a life of learning. Learn from success and learn from failure. Learn from every moment of experience. If knowledge is power, then learning is the fuel for the engine that gives the power to be Quality Leaders. Of utmost importance is that leaders use their learning skills to develop personal plans for the continuous improvement of self and organization.

Empathy is being able to feel what others are feeling. A Quality Leader does not sympathize with others but has true empathy for their state of existence. That empathy results in an ability to listen to not just what a person says but to the context and condition under which it is said. Empathic listening allows a leader to hear more than words, it allows the leader to hear the feeling that drives the ideas that the speaker is trying to convey. The empathic leader wants to know if what is being heard is what the speaker truly means. When empathic leadership is employed, most organizational conflicts disappear.

Attitude plays an important role for the Quality Student Leader. Nothing is impossible—some things are just more difficult to achieve. The quality attitude is one that believes that improvement is always possible, and quality leaders should benchmark themselves against the highest possible standards. This attitude also reveals that a dedicated individual can make a difference. Even though "I" am only one person with limited power and authority to make any significant changes, "I" realize that the greatest changes in the history of humankind have been instigated by people with relatively little, if any, formal authority to propose or generate change. Ghandi, King, and Mandela are just three of the names that quickly come to mind. These men propelled their respective societies toward dramatic change without the cloak of formal authority. Each of them had the quality attitude that led them to believe that life could be better for their people, and that it was their destiny to push on the system until it changed.

Dedication is at the core of Quality Student Leadership. Dedication is a sign of total commitment to an ideal. It takes a grasp of the all-or-nothing principle for leaders to make an impact on their organization. It is either a 100% commitment to achieve the goals, or it is being left up to chance. Without the dedication produced by a 100% commitment, doubt creeps into one's world. The uncertainty results in a hesitancy that, in turn, compromises quality. Without dedication, adequate preparation does not take place. Without adequate preparation, leaders have to rely on luck, and luck is nothing more than playing the odds. In most schools, the odds are that someone else will win if the members of that school community have not had the dedication needed to prepare. Quality Leaders are dedicated to the principle of continuous improvement and the creation of an environment of trust. They are also dedicated to the team that will help bring about the quality transformation needed in the organization.

Energy is not something you get, it's something you have. In the world of physics, students are taught that energy can neither be created nor destroyed. This is definitely true in the physical world, but in the world of Quality Student Leadership, energy grows and multiplies in relation to the level of dedication and in response to the attitude of the leader. The more dedicated a leader is, the more energy there is. Coupled with the Quality Student Leadership attitude, there is never a depletion of the energy as long as there is a focus on the goals to be achieved. Quality Leaders do not need catchy phrases or slogans to motivate them; they possess the energy of vision and dedication, and this motivates them to achieve the organization's goals. The Quality Student Leader also shares energy with everyone who needs it, zapping others to increase their energy and prop up their dedication. An amazing thing about the energy of Quality Leaders is that the more they share with others, the more they seem to have.

Respect for everyone without question is essential for Quality Student Leaders. If goals are to be achieved, it is necessary for everyone to work together as a team. Without respect, there is no team. Respect takes form in many ways. It shows others that leaders care, and that they believe in team members. Respect listens to divergent opinions and looks for the merits they possess. Respect focuses on similarities, not differences, yet it is always aware that people are different for many reasons. Differences allow for the creation of new ideas, products, and perspectives. Respect listens with empathy and checks to make sure the Quality Leader truly understands what the other person is saying. Respect is the recognition of human worth and dignity, which both exist without exception for all people.

Service is the vehicle by which Quality Student Leaders effect change in their world. Service means being of assistance or benefit to others. Leadership is only of value when it provides a service. Therefore, leaders must serve to be Quality Leaders. Service allows the leader to add quality and value to the organization and society as a whole. Leadership is never a drain on the leader, the organization, or the community. What should a leader do for others? Essentially, the Quality Leader helps others fulfill their own needs through the constructive participation in the work of the organization. A Quality Organization helps the community fulfill its needs through the work of the community. A Quality Community helps its citizens fulfill their needs in the most efficient and effective manner possible. These needs relate to being an integral part of the organization, having power over one's own destiny, being free to make the choices that one believes will have the greatest potential for achieving important goals, and being able to enjoy the entire process. This, of course, is beyond the basic human survival needs that must be met for all people. Quality Student Leaders are aware of all these needs and do what they can to help others meet these needs for themselves.

Honesty is not the best policy for Quality Student Leaders—it is the only policy. Quality Leaders are honest with themselves and with others. Each person needs to take a careful look at his or her standards and how daily performance compares to those standards. If leaders are truly honest, they will benchmark their personal standards against the highest quality standards possible. Some people might shy away from this, fearing that they will never match up, but not the Quality Student Leader. Quality Leaders embrace these high standards because they realize that their personal evaluation of their own performance is not based on attaining those standards but a directional movement with respect to those standards. Leaders are behaving in a Quality way when they move closer to the benchmark. Leaders only fail when they are moving away from their standards and fail to correct their course. Of course, leaders must make certain that their standards meet all of the characteristics of Quality Leadership and have not been set in a manner that detracts from any aspect of quality.

Ingenuity is the mark of the Quality Student Leader. There are many things left undone for want of a way to accomplish the task. It is the creativity and clevermindedness of Quality Leaders that sets them apart from others. The good news is that anyone can be a Quality Leader. It's not a hereditary trait. It does, however, require that leaders use their quality attitudes and remember that nothing is impossible, some tasks are just more difficult than others. To make what seems to be impossible, possible, most often requires that leaders look at the problem from a new angle. Many times, leaders are limited by their own view of the situation. Leaders need to create new tools, new methods, new procedures, and new opportunities so that they can break down the old problems into new challenges. The ingenuity of Quality Student Leaders allows them to do what seemed impossible.

Passion is the emotion of Quality Student Leaders. Their passion stems from their mission and is focused on the continuous improvement of their organization's ability to meet the needs of its members and its community. This passion drives them toward being better *learners* of what it takes to be a leader. This passion opens the heart and mind so that the leader can be empathic and adopt the *attitude* of possibilities. This passion allows the leaders to be *dedicated* to goals that *serve* all members of the organization and community, and it taps the wellspring of *energy* that is available to those who lead with *respect* for all. Finally, this passion knows the truth of *honesty* to self and others and has a *creative genius* that makes the impossible, possible. *Passion* is the driving force behind what makes a leader a Quality Student Leader.

Brief Overview of the Process

QSL is "a strategy for transforming our schools and communities through direct student involvement" (Goldman, 1990, p. A3). It is a unique process that integrates Quality Education, student leadership, and involvement, that is, the creation of schools of quality, true learning organizations, where everyone, adults and students alike, are dedicated to continuous improvement of people, processes, and systems. QSL emphasizes the development of the *innate leadership potential of every student* through a systematic and interactive process of self-esteem building, critical thinking and problem solving, team development, and action planning. It is a vital contributor to the student's educational path and is designed to enrich students, teachers, parents, and community in the development of a community of learning.

The objectives of QSL are

- To develop student leadership, self-esteem, and teamwork skills
- To develop self-directed learners who are achieving in school and life
- To increase student involvement in the school improvement process
- To encourage critical thinking for creative problem solving
- To develop interpersonal and intrapersonal relationship skills
- To increase student responsibility, decision making, and ownership in schools
- To provide opportunities to incorporate quality principles for personal and career development

- To involve students of all achievement levels, including challenged and at risk, in making a positive contribution to their school

- To train teachers, parents, community, and students to expand the QSL process in their schools and communities

Master Plan for Student Empowerment

There is a critical difference between a program and a process. A program is set in its structure and does not allow room for variation or change. A process is alive and dynamic, thus allowing for adaptation of each school community's unique needs. Accordingly, the QSL Master Plan for Student Empowerment is flexible and adaptable to each organization's unique needs and culture, because each would be in varying stages of its school improvement plan.

The starting place in the model may occur at different strategic places. A key element of the process is continuous improvement through the ongoing monitoring, course corrections, and interventions in all the Master Plan stages. The key components are commitment, assessment, awareness, planning, training, coaching, ongoing monitoring and evaluation, interventions, and recognition (see Figure 1.2). Specifically, the QSL training program flowchart starts with (a) team formation, and then moves to (b) training of adult/student teams, and (c) team goals and action plans that are focused on school/community improvement projects. The final stage, which can be built into prior stages, is (d) recognition and celebration of successes that validate the work completed. These components are woven together with real and practical strategies that provide a dynamically synergistic process for organizations.

There is a continuous amazement stemming from the creative exploration and variations that arise from introducing the Master Plan template to new clients. This is an important, and many times understated, part of the success of an initiative. When this creative spirit is allowed to flourish, there is an intrinsic buy-in to the whole process, because it comes from everyone involved. The idea of buy-in will be clarified as you progress through this book. It is a key to success.

For any initiative to work, relationships of trust must be continually built, sustained, and, at times, repaired. This is not an easy task, because there is often risk and hard work involved. That is where the partnership of an external consultant and internal stakeholders pro-

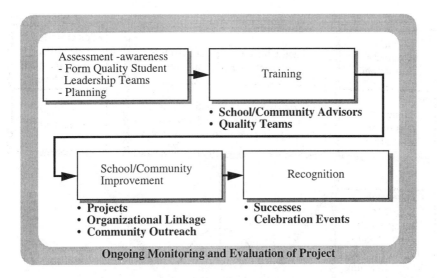

Figure 1.2. Comprehensive student leadership training program for school improvement.

vides a dynamic union. Many times, an outside source may see things more objectively and have more freedom to try new methods or strategies, because he or she is not involved with the cultural politics or norms. This will also be explored in more depth.

The QSL Master Plan for Student Empowerment flowchart (see Figure 1.3) is used as a generic template that can be revised and adapted to fit any organization's strategic direction and needs. Ensuing chapters will discuss real examples of projects that demonstrate how this model works in different situations.

1. Secure Principal's or Other Decision Maker's Commitment

This is an important step, in that without the instructional leader's full commitment to not only proceed, but to be involved and supportive of the process, it is very difficult to be successful. He or she sets the tone for the continuity and integrity of this school improvement effort. Other stakeholders, adults and students alike, will sense the leader's level of commitment and accordingly emulate it. Commitment means acting on a strategic direction, not just making a verbal affirmation. It means identifying key champions who will support and see the plan through in spite of obstacles. It means that the leader is there for the long run and will do whatever is required to make the process a success.

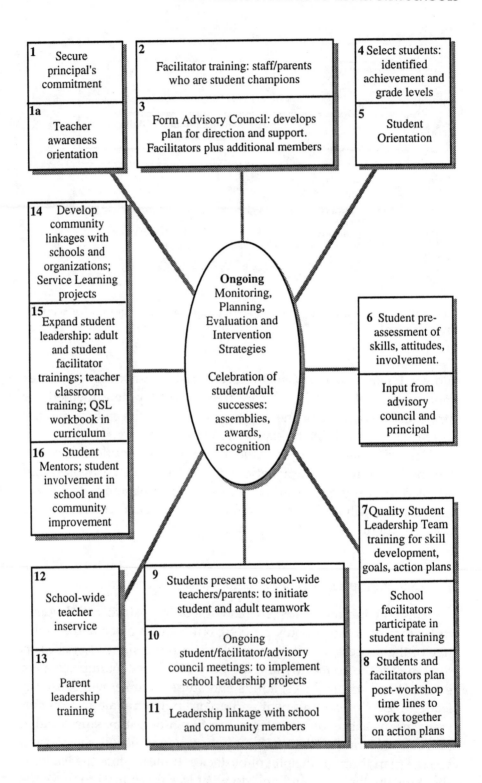

Figure 1.3. Master plan for student empowerment.

1a. Teacher Awareness Orientation

This step introduces the classroom instructional leaders, the teachers, to the overall purpose of the project and the key components. This serves several purposes. One purpose is that teachers have numerous programs "thrown" at them over and above their classroom teaching assignment. They are usually overloaded and overwhelmed by the multitude of mandates in their schools. There is usually some level of resistance to "another program." Doing an awareness orientation demonstrates that the administration values them as professionals who deserve to know about the program ahead of time and can give input to the process. A second purpose is that teachers know their classroom and school culture and can offer valuable ideas to ensure the success of the initiative. It is also good to know where and what resistance there may be in the school culture that could provide challenges to the program's success. A final purpose is to use the data obtained to fine tune the Master Plan process. Perhaps one of the greatest assets of the QSL process is that it is not a program. It is a strategy that can be used to confront one of the most pervasive problems facing schools today: noninvolvement.

Using an orientation to assess, from the teacher's point of view, the strengths and weaknesses of the school community is an excellent way to get buy-in. By asking the stakeholders what their real or perceived needs are, stakeholders understand that they are considered to be important cogs in the machinery of the school. A more extensive assessment could include a written questionnaire that teachers could submit anonymously in a sealed envelope to the consultants. The process has been able to elicit key school issues using this format that may have otherwise gone undetected.

2. Facilitator Training: Staff/Parent Student Champions

The purpose of training school facilitators is to begin the process of self-management, where internal champions are empowered to work directly with students. In this way, they share their knowledge with other stakeholders, such as teachers, staff, parents, and community. It has been found that school facilitators may need some support from consultants over a negotiated time period to really embed this process into the school culture. Each school is different, and the amount of time and type of support needed to ensure the cooperation and involvement of the school facilitators should be discussed thoroughly.

Another modification of this model is to train student facilitators or peer leaders to support other students. This can occur later in the process or in the early stages. One advantage of doing this is that students grow quickly when they are helping others. Of course, one has to review the school's culture to determine if the staff is open to this idea, and then address any and all concerns. Various school projects, where students are and have been involved, will be discussed in subsequent chapters.

The facilitator training demonstrates the principles of the QSL process. Theory is balanced with interactive exercises to give the participants an integrated experience and the readiness skills needed to develop student leaders in their school or community. Participants are given modules designed to provide practice in leadership skills and opportunities to work with others in the training and application of those skills. There is also a provision for time to reflect on the processes that assist participants in integrating and internalizing the information and group dynamics.

3. Form Advisory Council: Develops Plan for Direction and Support

An internal lead team for planning is essential in providing school-wide support. Team members are usually identified by the principal or other designated leader as key stakeholders in the school or organization. They can be a mix of teachers, counselors, parents, community members, and administration. Some schools are open to inviting a student representative. The idea is to have as many of the members of the school community represented as is reasonable and possible.

The specific mission of this lead team is manifold. This team will be responsible for

- Developing strategies for the effective implementation of the process in their school
- Clarifying aims and intended outcomes of the project
- Developing the logistics of the project
- Addressing challenges in human resources and relations, facilities, and the organization
- Ensuring continuous improvement and monitoring
- Linking the program components and goals to the school's School Improvement Plan goals
- Identifying the school project coordinator, champions, and department- or grade-level chairs

4. Select Students: Identified Achievement and Grade Levels

The principal or other organizational leader with the lead team will identify the students to be involved in the student leadership training. The criteria for selection need to be decided. They could include grade levels, student achievement, gender, racial and ethnic diversity, leadership potential, available time, and so on. A key to success for some schools has been that the leadership training has been inclusive rather than exclusive. Through the QSL process, nothing has been found to improve a school's culture faster than letting the disenfranchised be part of the franchise.

Having a clear school mission for the project will assist in the student selection process. If the mission is to empower the existing student leadership organizations, then students selected would most probably be the members or officers of these groups. If the mission is to provide a school culture of students of all achievement levels working together for success, then identified students may include formal and informal student leaders. A discussion of specific school models will be found in the later chapters to demonstrate this concept.

5. Student Orientation

The purpose of this step is to invite the students to commit to the program. This involves discussing the purpose of the program, why the students were selected, and student responsibilities and time needed; addressing questions; and asking for their commitment to participate. What this does is open a dialogue and demonstrate respect for the students as responsible individuals who can make intelligent choices. Rather than mandating, we are giving a unique opportunity to them, if they so choose. Once one makes an independent choice, then he or she is fully responsible for it. If one is forced to choose, then there is always the "out" of, "I didn't really want to do it. I was made to." The QSL experience is that when young people are given the same consideration as are adults, then they will make the proper and right decisions.

6. Student Preassessment: Skills, Attitudes, Involvement

This will provide baseline data for the students to be trained, and the data will identify real student strengths and weaknesses. The assessment can be custom designed by the school and its consultants, or an existing school tool can be used. It may be that a schoolwide

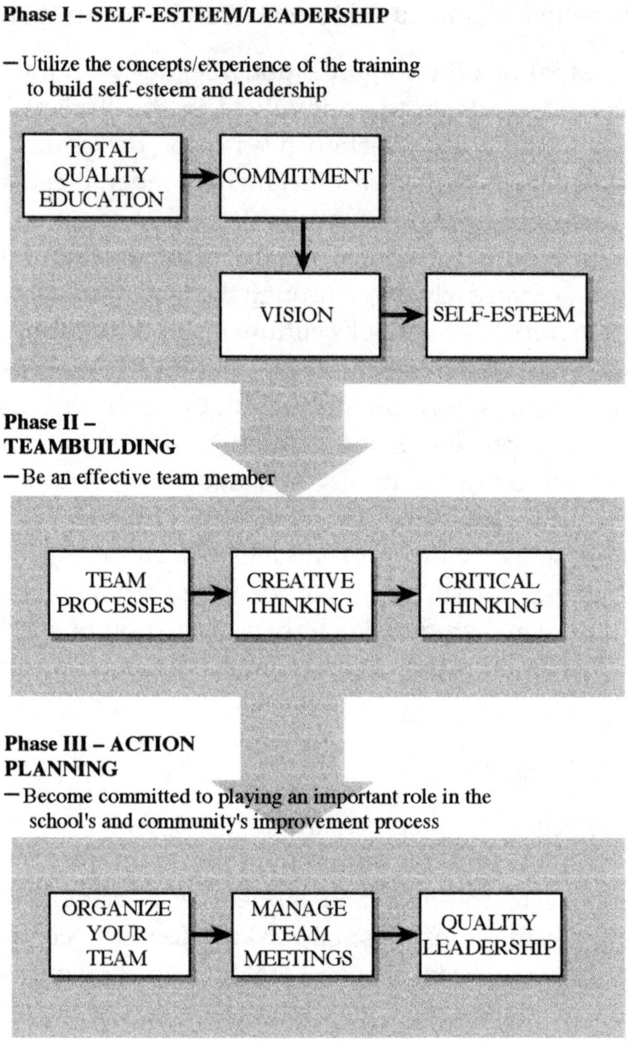

Phase I – SELF-ESTEEM/LEADERSHIP

—Utilize the concepts/experience of the training
to build self-esteem and leadership

```
┌──────────┐      ┌────────────┐
│  TOTAL   │      │            │
│ QUALITY  │ ───▶ │ COMMITMENT │
│EDUCATION │      │            │
└──────────┘      └────────────┘
                         │
                         ▼
                  ┌────────┐      ┌─────────────┐
                  │ VISION │ ───▶ │ SELF-ESTEEM │
                  └────────┘      └─────────────┘
```

**Phase II –
TEAMBUILDING**

—Be an effective team member

```
┌──────────┐      ┌──────────┐      ┌──────────┐
│  TEAM    │ ───▶ │ CREATIVE │ ───▶ │ CRITICAL │
│PROCESSES │      │ THINKING │      │ THINKING │
└──────────┘      └──────────┘      └──────────┘
```

**Phase III – ACTION
PLANNING**

—Become committed to playing an important role in the
school's and community's improvement process

```
┌──────────┐      ┌──────────┐      ┌────────────┐
│ ORGANIZE │      │  MANAGE  │      │            │
│   YOUR   │ ───▶ │   TEAM   │ ───▶ │  QUALITY   │
│   TEAM   │      │ MEETINGS │      │ LEADERSHIP │
└──────────┘      └──────────┘      └────────────┘
```

Figure 1.4. Quality Student Leadership process.

student assessment has already been done to show the big picture of
the entire student body. This can be helpful in seeing student trends
and patterns.

The QSL process has various assessment tools. One example that
aligns with Figure 1.4 (the three phases of QSL) is intrapersonal,
interpersonal, and action.

Once a preassessment is completed, then the QSL training will
integrate these data as a means of addressing the real student needs
and maximizing their strengths. (See Resource B for the complete
assessment.)

7. QSL Team Training for Skill Development, Goals, and Action Plans

This student leadership program is based on the philosophy that students of all achievement levels can learn and have leadership abilities. When this belief is acted on with the proper training and support, then every student will begin to demonstrate the positive traits of true leadership. The QSL training, as well as the QSL Master Plan, is a process that is flexible and can fit into a variety of settings: student councils; student leadership clubs; classrooms; challenged students (potential dropouts, low achievers, special education, gang and drug prevention); student and adult partnerships in school improvement; service learning; community youth organizations; and continuous quality improvement efforts.

The QSL process is divided into three phases (see Figure 1.4):

Phase I—Self-Esteem/Leadership: This phase uses the concepts associated with building self-esteem and leadership in the classroom, school, and community.

Phase II—Teambuilding: This phase creates effective team members using concepts associated with being an effective member of a group, committee, or organization.

Phase III—Action Planning: This phase helps the students to develop personal plans and set goals to become productive members of society. It also develops student commitment to playing an active role in the school's and community's improvement process.

These three phases have proven to be an effective strategy in building student involvement. Students need to develop a positive self-concept of believing in themselves and knowing that they can succeed. As they develop the decision-making skills needed for making productive choices, a solid foundation from which students can build relationships and teamwork skills is established. These relationship skills are necessary for students to be able to progress into working on goals, action plans, and real-life school and community projects. Integrated into these three phases are continuous improvement strategies that allow for the uniqueness of each school's culture.

7a. School Facilitators Participate in Student Leadership Training

Depending on the school and the goals of the project, adult facilitators can be involved in this stage. When the adults participate in the process with the students, they begin to internalize the concepts more readily and also "bond" with the student participants (and vice versa). As both stakeholder groups (students and adults) disclose personal visions and goals, as well as strengths and weaknesses, a greater appreciation on a human level emerges. This is invaluable for the program's long-term success and for trust and respect, and true caring builds relationships, both on the team and individually. As challenges come up, they are apt to be dealt with more readily, and mutual support will be the norm rather than the exception.

On the other hand, some student workshops may work better initially without adult attendance. The modus operandi for many adults is, "We are in control and know better." That kind of attitude will not work well in what we are trying to accomplish. The kind of attitude that is conducive is, "We want to participate on a cooperative basis, being open to student ideas as well as students being open to our ideas. We are in a continuous learning mode and are willing to share power." When the students see this occurring, they are most willing to contribute and work with the adults.

8. Students and Facilitators Plan Post-Workshop Timelines to Work Together on Action Plans

Putting the visions, goals, and plans into real school life action, beyond the QSL workshop, is the next step. As part of the QSL workshop's action-planning process, specific postworkshop timelines to put the action plans into motion are required. Many of the timelines may have been worked out prior to the workshop with the lead/ advisory team. If this is the case, then the student participants should be brought up-to-date on the logistics and invited to give their feedback on the feasibility of the timelines.

If the postworkshop timelines are being developed during the actual student workshop, then collaborative student/adult planning can be effective to get all viewpoints of all participants. This idea will secure greater buy-in and involvement. Criteria such as location of meetings; days; times (before, during, or after school); who's responsible for organizing, reminding, facilitating, monitoring, and reporting progress, need to be established. Different monitoring and reporting strategies will be shown later in the book.

9. Students Present to Schoolwide Teachers/Parents

This stage of the Master Plan was discovered through a workshop exercise that was designed to break down a school's cultural norms, which often separate students and adults and are grounded in old paradigms. It has been found that in many schools, students are not seen as capable of contributing to the school improvement efforts, and their ideas are not taken seriously, listened to, nor acted upon. When students who have gone through our QSL training are invited to present their vision, goals, and action plans to the entire faculty and/or parents, a newfound spirit—"we are important members of the school community"—is kindled. There is nothing like leadership in action to inspire and motivate young people. The effect on the adults can also be profound. When teachers and parents of these children see the students' commitment and the new skills being utilized, the teachers and parents are taken to a new level of commitment and openness to the possibilities of what students can do. Many times, there is shared dialogue, where real, honest communication is given and received. Many times, it is the adults who are talking and the students who are listening (or at least pretending to). When there is shared communication, then a powerful opening to create community is started.

10. Ongoing Student/Facilitator/Advisory Council Meetings to Implement School Leadership Projects

To create a cultural change where students are included in the transformation of our schools and communities, ongoing, consistent meetings need to occur. These meetings are a vital way of building effective teamwork, sharing progress of projects, monitoring and providing appropriate interventions to keep on course, and continuing to evaluate and identify success strategies and outcomes. An accountability mechanism is needed to ensure ongoing involvement and tracking of the above areas. These projects may be classroom, school, or community based, and they may be solely with students or with collaboration among students and adults. Examples of this will be discussed.

11. Student Leadership Linkage With Student Body

Student leaders can influence their peers more readily than adults can. That is one reason to involve students of all achievement levels in leadership training. Students who have experienced certain challenges in their education and life can easily relate to their peers, whether high achievers or low achievers. For student involvement to grow throughout the school culture, students need to be part of the process through modeling, coaching, and team leadership in the classroom, school, and community.

12. Schoolwide Teacher Inservices

For a true cultural change to occur, where adults and students are in a cooperative partnership, teachers need to be informed. Providing staff development in the areas of student leadership and empowerment, empowering students as learners, quality leadership, student motivation, positive discipline, conflict prevention, and creating student/adult teamwork will help to establish a philosophical base on which all other improvements can be made. Teachers are the vital link to encouraging students to succeed. They can assist in bringing the classroom alive through connecting academics and key life skills that can be translated into real-life situations and relevant learning.

Many teachers are looking for innovative methods to reach their students, where they are being self-directed learners and responsible for themselves. The work we do accomplishes this so that students can take these behaviors not only into the classroom, but also into the school and community. A new paradigm has to replace the old one. In this new paradigm, students are challenged to their highest potential, not as a meaningless mandate but in a renewed spirit of respect for each student's uniqueness and ability to contribute to the school.

13. Parent Leadership Training and Involvement

Parent involvement is a key element in creating a school community where students are empowered as learners and leaders. Parents need to feel that they are a part of the school community team and that they are working in partnership with the teachers. It is a vital partnership that is missing in many of our schools. The school can do only so much as the "extended family." This parent component works in four areas: (a) Realize your full potential, (b) build self-esteem for success with children, (c) work as a family team, and (d) make a difference in your school and community. The QSL process has shown that when students are enthused and have "ownership" in their educational process, parents will want to be more involved in their schools.

14. Develop Community Linkages With Schools and Organizations: Service Learning Projects

The school is central to a healthy and thriving community. Schools need to develop partnerships with all facets of the community: business and industry, health care organizations, community organizations, religious organizations, local government agencies, police, universities, and others. Students can become involved in many of these

community linkages: entrepreneurial initiatives for career and economic development; building higher order thinking skills to solve real
problems; school-to-work initiatives to learn to be competitive in the
job market; church and recreational youth involvement; service to
child care and elder centers; interface with local, state, and national
government youth development efforts; new school and community
improvement projects; and so on.

Service learning is a whole new area of exploration with students
where they learn and use new skills in real-world projects. Another
important component is reflection on what the students really learned
that they can apply in their school and life. Service learning also links
to the curriculum to integrate the key elements of academic disciplines
with practical life problem solving.

15. Expand Student Leadership: Adult and Student Facilitator Trainings, Teacher Classroom Training, QSL Workbook in Curriculum

QSL is an ongoing process that is intended to promote a positive
cultural change in the school community. The process is designed to
become self-perpetuating and eventually self-managing. For this to
occur, more school stakeholders need to be trained as facilitators of
the process. Ideally, a student/adult partnership works to ensure
increased involvement of adults and students throughout the school.

The integration of academic and life skills in the classroom and
school are vital to an authentic learning environment. Today, more
than ever, young people need to have those life/career skills of teamwork, leadership, problem solving, self-directed learning, building
effective relationships, communication, goal-setting, and creative
thinking.

The comprehensive QSL workbook and guide provides a model
to follow, not only for school and community student leadership but
for classroom leadership and learning. The QSL learning guide further
promotes the schoolwide cultural impact of these school life skills for
students, teachers, and parents alike.

16. Student Mentors, Student Involvement in School and Community Improvement

Mentoring is an important part of learning and growing. Throughout life, all of us will have had mentors that assisted us in some way.
Students who become mentors for their peers are involved in a wonderful learning opportunity. Their leadership skills are put into a
positive and powerful forum for service. Numerous schools have seen

students serve as mentors for other students their own age or across grade levels. Student-to-student programs have allowed high school students to set a positive example for their peers or for younger, less advantaged youth. In either case, the outcome is as beneficial for the mentor as it is for the mentee.

Ultimately, we are talking about involving students as partners in improving our schools and communities. What an exciting concept! For some, this can be threatening; others are open but not sure how to accomplish this. Finally, there are those who have tried various strategies to involve students and have had some success but are looking for new support vehicles to build on what has worked.

Ongoing: Monitoring, Planning, and Intervention Strategies (Internal and External)

Through the initial planning process (Step 3), these elements need to be discussed with specific program outcomes in mind. The monitoring, continuous planning, and interventions will support this outcome becoming a reality. Ideally, a collaborative effort of school (internal) and community (external) efforts will maximize the ongoing program success. This provides a perspective to the school that may not be visible from within.

"Ongoing" is one of the key ideas. As was discussed earlier, QSL is a process in which there is continual assessment of what is working and what needs improvement or elimination. This can be accomplished only with a clear commitment from the participants—individually, team, and schoolwide. Various methods of accomplishing this will be shared in real project examples.

Celebration of Student/Adult Successes

Recognizing and celebrating successes, whether large or small, is an often-overlooked part of the process. It is key because all organizations need to take time to acknowledge success. Many times, schools get into the habit of looking at what didn't work, or they just keep on doing and doing.

Both of these approaches will eventually wear people out, causing burnout. In our work, we continually acknowledge people—adults and students—for their simple and larger contributions. The power this has to revitalize and increase the commitment of the participants is amazing. Celebrating people can be done in inservices, assemblies, special events or dinners, posting up, intercom announcements, plaques, and so on. The ways are numerous.

2

Making Commitments and Sharing the Vision

Until one is committed there is hesitancy, the chance to draw back, always ineffectiveness. Concerning all acts of initiative (and creation), there is one elementary truth, the ignorance of which kills countless ideas and splendid plans; that the moment one definitely commits oneself, then Providence moves too.

All sorts of things occur to help one that would never otherwise have occurred. A whole stream of events issues from the decision, raising in one's favour all manner of unforeseen incidents and meetings and material assistance, which no man could have dreamt would have come his way. I have learned a deep respect for one of Goethe's couplets:

> Whatever you can do, or dream you can, begin it.
> Boldness has genius, power, and magic in it.

(Goethe, as quoted in Goldman, 1990, p. B7)

Before any endeavor can become a success, it is essential that all stakeholders are committed to the goal. This commitment cannot be halfhearted. Success requires a full, 100% commitment to the project. If most people examine their own lives and find goals they have achieved, they will find an undaunted spirit and total commitment behind that success. What is achieved easily rarely has lasting, fulfilling space in the heart. But oh, when experiences have tested the mettle of the passionate, and they found themselves up to the task, those are memories cherished forever.

This chapter is titled "Making Commitments and Sharing the Vision." These commitments are commitments that adhere to the all-or-nothing principle. The all-or-nothing principle has been borrowed from neurobiology. The basic concept is that a neuron is either stimulated or it is not. There are no halfway neurological impulses. If sufficient stimulation of a neuron does not occur, nothing happens, and once that level of stimulation has been reached, no additional stimulation can make the neurological impulse be any stronger or happen any faster. The power of the stimulation is dependent on the number of neurons stimulated. Such is the manner of commitment. Unless there is sufficient commitment, there will be no movement toward our goal. Yet once sufficient commitment for goal achievement has been reached, a greater commitment will not accelerate the process, and should the commitment level drop, progress will also drop. The only factor that will influence the rate of success is the number of people committed to the project.

An additional factor to consider, which fits well with the neurological metaphor, is the danger of overstimulation. With the human nervous system, stimulating the same set of nerves for an excessive period of time can result in a temporary paralysis of that anatomical region. We most often notice this as a numbness and think of this as that part of our body having gone to sleep. Most of us can relate to that event. An organization can experience very similar effects if members are asked to remain committed to a single action or goal for too long a period of time without rest. To be single-minded in our efforts and commitment is essential for achieving important goals, but it is just as important to allow time for recreating that commitment. This latter phenomenon is becoming very evident in school organizations in which heavy emphasis and strong efforts have been focused on school improvement.

Many of the best and most productive schools have hit periods of paralysis. It is important for schools to recognize the signs of impending disaster and provide the opportunity to take a few steps back, put the commitment in a temporary resting place, and allow team members to take a vacation. After such a respite, the team can come back to the commitment with a renewed vigor and sense of purpose.

The greatest enemy of transforming our schools into "Total Quality Schools," however, is not experiencing overstimulation of the commitment centers. It is just the opposite. Too many schools are having difficulty garnering the commitment necessary to begin making the transformation. How do schools go about engendering the type of commitment and support necessary to create the culture for change? The most fundamental principle is inclusion. All stakeholders in the process need to feel as though they have a "voice and a choice"— that is, that they will be listened to and made partners in the decision-making process.

In working with an extremely diverse sample of students from around the country, it has been found that a starting point is to get students talking about what they really want from school. Wherever efforts to transform schools have been made, whether it is the cornfields of Iowa, the projects in Chicago, the beaches of Florida and California, or the fruit orchards of western Michigan, students have generally had the same wants, hopes, and desires about education. The following vision was created by high-risk students at an "At-Risk" conference in Des Moines, Iowa. Although it was developed by students from a fairly rural background, it could have just as easily been written by students from an inner-city high school in Chicago. Their vision for student involvement was the following:

> We believe that we can make a difference through cooperation, determination, initiative, organization, and opportunity. We can use our leadership to accomplish our goal to change student roles and attitudes. By working together, building each other up and utilizing our individual strengths, we can accomplish our realistic goals and say, "We did something!"

This vision created the beginning of a commitment. It is important, as follow-up, for the vision to be nurtured and supported. Therefore, each of these students met with advisors who would be taking the students back to their own schools and helping them begin to implement their vision.

The commitment facilitated by the vision is the first step on a long road of continuous improvement. To keep the commitment fresh requires that we focus that commitment on a specific goal to be achieved. If the nature of the vision is allowed to remain too general, it will tarnish and falter. Therefore, the next step in nurturing this visionary commitment to student involvement is to develop an achievable goal that will move the school toward the vision.

Once teams are committed to a vision, it is important to identify some specific goals to work toward that are consistent with that vision. This can be done by having individuals identify their own goals in relation to the vision. Next, they can share them with the team and then create team goals that will help meet the needs of all team members and nurture the vision. It can also be helpful to have team members commit to some basic operational guidelines. Some that have worked extremely well in the past have been the following:

1. Be on time.
2. Participate 100%.
3. Be willing to take positive risks.
4. Take full responsibility for what you do.

These guidelines have made for some interesting discussions, especially the last one. In our Des Moines, Iowa, workshop, one of the students stated that he was not willing to take responsibility for what he did. He let everyone know that it would make him have to think about what he was doing before he did it. This was very insightful and, of course, led to a greater commitment on the part of the entire group.

The methods of the Quality Student Leadership (QSL) program help participants make important commitments to their school and community. One of the best ways to demonstrate this is through direct quotations from students. A senior student leader from Sturgis High School in Sturgis, Michigan, says:

> I hope more students will get involved and get into this program. Anyone can join in and I encourage [students] to try it. This year we have many more students than last year and we could always use more. We need community support and parental support so I hope our students will also get their families involved. This year is going great and I hope it will continue. *I plan on coming back, even after I graduate.*

Participants are encouraged to keep a leadership journal that helps to document skill development and keep track of what works. By identifying growth and success, commitment grows.

Another tool for helping team members make a greater commitment is to have them do some self-evaluation. Asking participants to identify agreements that they have both kept and broken, and having them explain what they think and feel about those situations, leads them to make a stronger commitment toward the team. The process of self-evaluation, accompanied by plans for improvement, is the most powerful commitment builder we have found. Self-evaluation is also consistent with the principles of Total Quality.

It has also been found that the greatest commitments occur on activities that are consistent with a person's own philosophy and goals for the future. Therefore, it can be very helpful, when you are attempting to garner commitments toward a certain project, to have team members examine their own goals. If a person can see how a project relates to his or her own goals, it will be much easier to make the commitment needed to move the project forward. For this reason, it is advantageous to have a variety of projects with which participants can become involved. This will increase the chances that a match between personal and organizational goals will occur.

Creating a Vision

Personal, Team, and Organizational Visions, Missions, and Goals

> Great men have been compared to giants upon whose shoulders pygmies have climbed, who nevertheless see further than they. (Claude Bernard, 1865, as quoted in Seldes, 1985)

A vision is a description of your personal, team, or organization's preferred future state. We recognize where we are and dream about where we would like to be. A vision is a dream translated into attainable form. It will lead to specific goals and outcomes that will drive you, your team, or your organization on a journey toward a higher existence. Our vision represents the big picture of our lives in terms that have relevance to what we want and hope to become. When all members of a school community agree on a vision, that vision drives the change and helps to promote improvement. It directs efforts and serves as an inspiration to staff, students, parents, and community. Of course, in application, it might be impossible to find an organization in which there is 100% agreement on anything, and it is in the details of planning to achieve a vision that disagreements occur. If the majority of people agree on the vision, validate the importance of diverse thoughts, and are considerate of the needs of the minority, the vision can still move the organization toward quality. In this way, it can be recognized that in diversity lies strength.

As a nation, it would be most beneficial if we had a common vision for education. We would like to suggest one that everyone could rally around. How about a vision of schools where:

> Everyone is a student and everyone is a teacher. In our schools, everyone learns all of the knowledge, skills, and abilities necessary for him or her to be a productive citizen. In our schools, everyone has the responsibility to help make the system work for the good of all students and teachers.

Now the question of "How do we make this happen?" can be answered. That is where more specific missions, goals, and objectives will help. It must, however, start with a vision that recognizes one fundamental, universal rule of planning: You will never be greater than the vision that guides you.

Personal visions get to the very heart of a person's beliefs and values. What people feel in their hearts will direct what they envision for their future. The same can be said for organizations. There is a heart and character of each organization. "When there is a genuine vision (as opposed to the all-too-familiar 'vision statement'), people excel and learn, not because they are told to, but because they want to" (Senge, 1990, p. 51). Think of this as the organization's culture. The organizational vision will be created based on that organization's collective beliefs and values, which will affect organizational politics, norms and shared practices, rituals, traditions, attitudes, interaction, and other aspects of organizational life.

To be consistent with the ethic of continuous improvement, the organization needs to review continually its vision and the paradigms that drive that vision. The organization must clarify its culture and make certain that it does not become paralyzed by an inability to experience a paradigm shift. It is imperative that organization members not fall into a rut that leads to resembling the people described by the great painter Picasso: "Anything new, anything worth doing, can't be recognized. People just don't have that much vision" (Seldes, 1985, p. 329). The vision must be a living vision. It must be revisited, and an organization's efforts must be filtered through that continually renewed vision.

The Mission

When an organization has a clear vision of where it wants to go and what it wants to be, its next step is to translate that vision into a clear and focused mission statement. If we use the vision stated above, we can create a mission that motivates the organization. That vision said:

> Everyone is a student and everyone is a teacher. In our schools, everyone learns all of the knowledge, skills, and abilities necessary for him or her to be a productive citizen. In our schools, everyone has the responsibility to help make the system work for the good of all students and teachers.

Considering this vision, we can create a mission that gives us a more specific plan for making the vision a reality. A possible mission might be the following:

> In partnership with parents, community, teachers, administrators, support staff members, and students, our schools will assist each student in acquiring the knowledge, skills, and abilities necessary to become a productive citizen and member of our community.

This mission becomes the foundation for the pragmatic steps that the school will take in an effort to make the dream a reality. The vision is marvelous but does not give a clue as to what is to be done. The mission provides the first glimpse into who will be involved and what will be done.

Even though the mission statement is more specific than the vision, it still does not give us an implementable plan for creating the school of that vision. To do this, stakeholders will need to know what processes will help them achieve their desired outcomes. They need to have a much clearer picture of exactly what those outcomes look like. Therefore, from the mission, schools must move to statements of desired outcomes that reflect the overall vision of what a student should become. These outcomes can either be cognitive or affective in nature. They deal with concrete facts and skills or abstract processes and abilities. Some will be easily measured, whereas others will be very difficult to measure. Unlike the minimal competencies of the past, these outcomes will be geared toward the optimization of each student's knowledge, skills, and abilities so they can be the most productive citizens possible.

Outcomes

Various states have come to their own conclusions as to what the outcomes of school should be. To give a universal picture of outcomes, there is one source for many of these state initiatives. That source is the *SCANS Report*. SCANS is an acronym for Secretary of Labor's Commission on Achieving Necessary Skills. The SCANS Commission was established by the Department of Labor to define what the specific needs of tomorrow's workplace will be. This report identified five areas of major competencies that have a three-part foundation.

The identified competencies are in the following areas:

1. Resources: Identifies, organizes, and allocates resources, such as time, money, materials, and people
2. Interpersonal: Works with others, that is, works on a team, teaches others new skills, works to satisfy the client's/customer's expectations, exercises leadership, negotiates, and works with diversity
3. Information: Acquires and uses information
4. Systems: Understands complex interrelationships, which means understanding systems, monitoring and correcting performance, and improving and/or designing systems
5. Technology: Works with a variety of technologies, selects proper technology for a task, applies the technology to the task, and maintains and troubleshoots equipment

These five areas for competency must be grounded upon a three-part foundation. These three parts are the following:

1. The basic skills of reading, writing, mathematics, speaking, and listening
2. Thinking skills such as creative thinking, decision making, problem solving, seeing the big picture, knowing how to learn, and reasoning
3. Personal qualities: Displaying responsibility, self-esteem, sociability, self-management, integrity, and honesty.

Truly, we would be remiss if we did not say that we must develop the whole child. To focus purely on the academic and intellectual skills and ignore the physical, emotional, social, and spiritual needs of our young people would generate no fundamental change in the student or the school and society as a whole. Where an individual fits into the larger scheme of our world and universe, to recognize that there is a greater good to which we are all ultimately held accountable—this must be the foundation of these personal qualities (SCANS, 1991).

When the five competencies are developed through the use of the three-part foundation, an overall set of expected outcomes can be established that contributes to students becoming skilled and literate worker-citizens.

The QSL Master Plan for student empowerment, discussed in Chapter 1, has been designed to address this three-part foundation. The entire student training process focuses on the acquisition of the communication, reasoning, thinking, problem-solving, and decision-making skills that the *SCANS Report* has identified as being critical for student success. Furthermore, through the 16 steps of the Master Plan, students are given ample opportunities to develop the personal qualities of responsibility, self-esteem, sociability, self-management, integrity, and honesty.

Goals

When a comprehensive school program is created around these principles and in conjunction with the concepts of Total Quality, it becomes possible to identify specific goals. These goals can drive the daily efforts of education and continuous school improvement. Through the QSL program, participants have several opportunities to improve their goal-setting skills. When the goals set are related back to the vision and mission, and when those goals are developed within the context of the competencies and foundations discussed above, goals take on a new meaning and dimension.

As you know, some goals are achieved, and others are not. What makes some goals more reachable than others? We believe that successful goal achievement depends more on the process of goal development than it does on the worthiness of the goal. Goal setting for success involves stating goals in positive statements and making sure that the goal is exciting and imaginable. Because most organizational goals are not met in just a few days and can often take weeks, months, or years to accomplish, it is necessary to update goals on a regular basis. Furthermore, the goals developed should meet five conditions. A success-oriented goal is specific, measurable, attainable, realistic, and trackable. This can be remembered through the acronym SMART.

It is also helpful to have a time limit for the achievement of goals. When goals drag out, interest wanes and the system generally breaks down. To increase the chances for successful goal achievement, it is important to have a clear mental picture of what is to be attained. Successful achievers often have such an intense focus on the goal that they can almost see, hear, feel, taste, and smell the outcome before the plan has been fully conceived. When an emotional lean toward this outcome is added, a highly positive attitude results. This attitude about the eventual product assists in the affirmation of the worth of the outcome and reinforcement for the belief that it will be a successful experience.

Using a goal derived from the expectations cited in the *SCANS Report*, the system of successful goal setting becomes more evident. Perhaps an academic goal is to have students write and present a persuasive speech that leads fellow students to be more tolerant of people with diverse cultural backgrounds. This goal will use several competencies and is grounded in all three parts of the foundations for education, as discussed in the *SCANS Report*. We also see that the goal is specific and is easily measurable using a scoring rubric for speeches. The first part of the goal is attainable, but the second part is somewhat more difficult. To actually lead students toward a greater tolerance for diversity is much more easily said than done, but in this case, it is probably a worthy cause. This is a realistic goal in that schools already require students to prepare oral presentations on a variety of topics. This goal simply addresses some of the issues raised in the *SCANS Report*. Finally, the goal is trackable. We can observe the impact of these speech experiences on students based on the number of incidents involving intolerance over a specific period of time.

This, then, brings up the time element. As with all educational goals, there truly is a multidimensional time frame. The actual speech preparation and presentation can be conducted over a 2-week period but the impact of those speeches on tolerance for diversity will take a greater amount of time for follow-up measures. An improvement team might want to say that it will measure the number of incidents of intolerance over a period of 3 months following the speeches, or set some other finite measurement timeline. In any case, there are several ways to bring the time element into the goal-setting process.

The measurement of progress toward goals can create some unique problems when you consider that so much of what educators are trying to do exists in a realm of intangibles. Primarily, teachers and administrators want to see students behave more responsibly, maintain a positive attitude, and desire truth and knowledge. To measure progress toward these more intangible goals, it is necessary to know what people do when they are exhibiting these qualities. How do they behave? How do they interact with others? What causes do they support? When the answers to these questions are known, observations of those behaviors in students can be used as indirect evidence that they have acquired these intangible skills and attitudes. It should be noted, however, that the attitude may not always follow the action. It is entirely possible that a person might behave in a certain way based on some other value. It must be understood that we may never be able to ascertain exactly what another person is thinking. Therefore, the goal should be to focus on the behavior rather than the actual attitude.

Measuring progress toward goals can be assisted through the use of several tools. Charts, graphs, and data tables are a few tools that can help visualize progress. They can also show long-range trends and will help shift the focus away from minor point fluctuations. These occur from time to time in all organizations and describe specific, time-related conditions rather than ongoing growth and development. For example, if a school wants to determine whether or not students are becoming more responsible, they might look for evidence of increased promptness, work completion, and willingness to contribute toward organizational goals. They may not know with certainty that a student's attitude has changed, but if the behavior improves, the school's atmosphere improves. An improved atmosphere becomes a measure of the quality of the culture, which, in turn, signifies an improving quality in the school.

It might be stated that goals function in both direct and indirect ways. Some goals will create very specific improvements in the intended domain, whereas others will affect a related area that can be interpreted as having an impact on the intended domain. It is important to realize that either approach is not only acceptable but must, for all practical purposes, be the mode of operation. In all cases, goals help to drive the continuous improvement of any organization.

Application of the Commitment and Visioning Process

In this and the following section, schools from dramatically different settings are discussed. The first is an inner-city high school attended primarily by minority students. The second is a group of schools located in rural northwest Iowa primarily attended by white, Anglo-Saxon, Protestant students. Even with this great difference between populations, the process was powerful for both groups.

In the practical application of the visioning process, students and teachers have demonstrated how they can affect a school's culture positively. Through a commitment of time and energy, young leaders, with the guidance of adult champions, can learn how to make a difference. In one inner-city high school, students made the decision to improve the quality of life and education for all students. The results

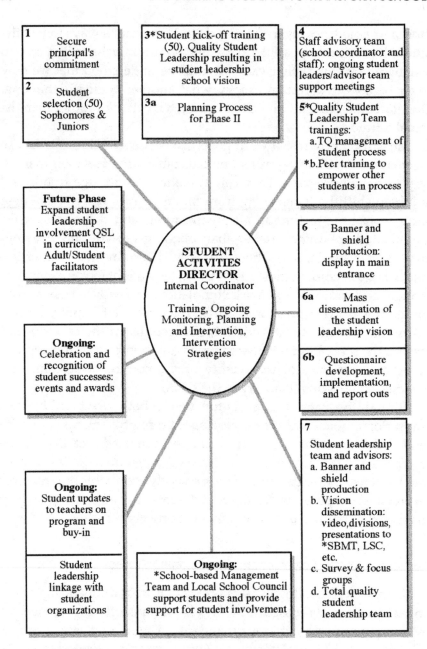

Figure 2.1. Master plan for student empowerment.
Note: Phase 1 = 1-3, Phase 2 = 4-7.
*Training

were nothing short of phenomenal (see Figure 2.1). It should be noted that here we are focusing on phases 1–3 of this Master Plan.

This inner-city high school must accept all students who wish to attend and who come from its attendance area. A majority of the students perform well below national averages at the time of admission. This school is charged with overcoming the overwhelming odds of increasing student achievement following 8 years of poor preparation. More than 65% of the student population is classified as low income, and many receive public aid, live in foster homes, or reside in institutions for delinquent children. Crime statistics in this school neighborhood are very high. Life in this inner-city school community can be very difficult for these students.

School authorities (Box 1 in Figure 2.1) invited QSL trainers to develop a student leadership and involvement program. The principal had hired a full-time, internal student activities director (center of Figure 2.1) who would help champion students. Fifty potential student leaders (Boxes 1, 2, and 3 in Figure 2.1), from all achievement levels, went through a 1-day training program in esteem, teamwork, and leadership. As a result, the students developed a powerful student leadership school vision:

STUDENT LEADERSHIP VISION

WE, THE STUDENTS . . ., HAVE IMPORTANT DREAMS THAT NEED TO BE FILLED. TAKE THE TIME AND THE PRIDE TO BE ALL YOU CAN BE. WITH THE RESPECT OF ONE ANOTHER, WE CAN PREPARE FOR A BRIGHTER FUTURE. WITH ALL OF THIS, THIS SCHOOL . . . WILL HAVE UNITY, HOPE, FAITH, TRUST, SPIRIT, AND PEACE. WITH LEADERSHIP AND DEDICATION THE VISION . . . WILL BECOME A REALITY.

This vision came out of the brainstorming exercise where the students were asked to verbally give key words that represented their ideal student vision for their school. An ad hoc group of 10 students volunteered to work on the student leadership school vision in a separate room to mold the vision into a complete and fluid statement. This group worked for an hour with a facilitator while the other students were doing an exercise. You could feel the air of expectancy when the student vision was read aloud. The entire group had begun to function as a team.

The students were a diverse group that needed to be constantly challenged to reach for new heights. One student in particular appeared to be uninvolved, and for a good part of the session, he had his head down on the desk. An important part of what we do is recognizing the subtle signals that students put out to determine what is really going on with them. We determined that he was listening to what was occurring, and we did not confront him to "straighten up." In another situation, an entirely different strategy might have been attempted. This student had included himself in the ad hoc group but did his own vision separately. He called it a "declaration." It is as follows:

A DECLARATION OF INDEPENDENCE

WHEN IN THE COURSE OF HIGH SCHOOL EVENTS, LOTS OF CHANGES GO FORTH IN OUR LIVES. WE MUST FOLLOW OUR DREAMS, LOOK FOR THE UNIQUE GOALS IN OUR LIVES. TO EXPLORE THE SOULS OF OUR STUDENTS. TO GIVE THEM A BRIGHT FUTURE. WE WANT A PEACE OF MIND, A TYPE OF UNITY IN OUR FAMILY.

WE MUST LEARN TO HAVE BETTER COMMUNICATION AMONG EACH OTHER. LET SUCCESS BE OUR NUMBER ONE PRIORITY. LET EDUCATION TAKE US FURTHER LIFE. TRY TO BE ALL WE CAN BE, AND FIND HAPPINESS IN ALL THAT WE MIGHT DO. LET US HAVE A FORM OF DEPENDABILITY, WORK TOGETHER, AND FIND MOTIVATION TO PUSH FOR-WARD. GIVE EACH OTHER MUTUAL RESPECT, WHICH WILL GIVE US FAITH AND SELF-ESTEEM IN ONE ANOTHER.

LEARNING TO UNDERSTAND ONE ANOTHER, OUR ACHIEVEMENTS. OUR KNOWLEDGE. OUR SPIRIT. LET US ALL MAKE A SACRIFICE, AND HOPE THAT WE CAN TRUST, AND BELIEVE IN ONE ANOTHER. EACH AND EVERY PER-SON IS LIKABLE, AND UNIQUE. THROUGHOUT OUR LIVES WE'VE HAD JOYOUS TIMES, AND TIMES OF PAIN. LET KNOWLEDGE BE POWER. LET THE STUDENTS OF . . . HIGH SCHOOL SAY, "A POWERFUL SOURCE OF LEADERSHIP WILL RISE AMONG US!" AND THE SPIRIT OF . . . WILL NEVER VANISH FROM OUR LIVES, BUT WILL GROW FOR YEARS TO COME . . .

. . . A STUDENT

A very inspiring vision, indeed! This experience, with this student, touches the very heart of the message in this book. There is a vast potential, largely untouched in young people, that must be tapped.

For what is waiting to be discovered is the richness of the future—children's minds, hearts, and spirit. If the wrong key (approach) is used to try to open that door, it will not open. But if the community dares to experiment with new approaches, the rewards are magnificent.

Rural Learning Collaborative Model Project

Since 1993, the Northwest Iowa Rural Learning Collaborative, representing 20 school districts, Iowa Lakes Community College, and Lakeland Area Education Agency (AEA), has worked in a special cross-school district event involving 15 high schools in a pilot project sponsored by the New Iowa School Development Corporation (see Figure 2.2). In 1992, school administrative leaders in the Lakeland AEA asked the question, "What can we do better together than we can do alone?" One of the answers was to create a regional learning center. This learning center is not a place; instead, it is a school without walls. The development of interdependent regional learning centers was called the "Galaxy Plan." The pilot was built around interdisciplinary teams of teachers working together to identify a relevant, real-life, community-based problem and then working with their communities to solve the problem. Instead of having teachers plan the community-based projects, students were asked to determine the relevant problem and to take responsibility for their own learning. Each identified problem centered on students' learning processes and skills instead of the traditional content approach. The interdisciplinary teams, too, were nontraditional because the composition of the teams all varied and included science, math, art, English, media, history, and vocational education staff.

In addition, teams were encouraged to use distance-learning technologies, including Iowanet, Internet, and Iowa Communications Network (fiber optics), to find possible solutions from other experts around the country. In addition, they worked internally to share information with other high schools on processes of how to go about finding information. The students were involved in the leadership training from the start in 1993. Student-teacher teams were invited from the 15 schools, which resulted in a participant population of about 100. This QSL training's purpose was to create an environment in schools that would allow students to get involved in curriculum planning and problem solving. The goal for the students was to build quality for themselves, their schools, and their communities. Each school created a student leadership vision, developed teamwork

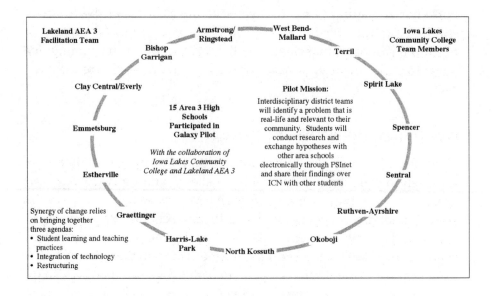

Figure 2.2. The Galaxy Plan.

skills, and expanded the role of shared leadership and decision making; from this, each school took the initiative to create action plans for solving the problem they identified. These initiatives were highly successful.

Numerous projects were developed that put students into contact with many aspects of their community, region, and state. Students engaged in statewide river testing, secured $175,000 in funding to dredge a local lake, successfully put through a school reorganization plan, built a teen center, started an inventions class, and taught myriad community members how to use technology. A key learning from the project was that projects were successful only if institutionalized, and that the principal was instrumental in making that happen. By the third year, the principals were part of the teams. In the big picture, the schools learned that three types of in-depth, ongoing leadership training were needed: Training was needed for principals, teachers, and students. Each of these groups needed improvement in facilitation, collaboration, action planning, action research, and data collection.

The successful implementation of this project has created an awareness of what schools can become and how all students can learn the skills, knowledge, and competencies to meet world-class standards. The Galaxy Plan has just begun. With student acquisition of these skills, with community and business involvement, and with the partnerships developed in the collaborative, a climate for economic development can thrive. As the project director for the Galaxy Plan stated,

> Area superintendents, principals, staff, and students all feel this is the most exciting and beneficial pilot with which they have ever been associated. It is helping all involved in our goals of adding quality to our curriculum. Even our at-risk students have changed their entire way of acting and became thoughtful builders of community.

The student leadership team vision (15 schools) is as follows:

> Our vision is to bring discipline and unity into our schools with a strong determination to succeed in all of our goals. In cooperation with the schools and the community, we will achieve these goals of freedom, respect, and commitment, and instill a new found pride in ourselves and each other.

Examples of individual school district team visions were the following:

- Our vision is to prepare responsible and productive citizens for an ever changing world by the utilization of our total resources through student leadership and involvement that would allow all students to reach their potential and excel in all their goals with a partnership of family, school, and community.
- It is the responsibility of all students to work cooperatively for a quality global education.
- We believe that students and faculty can work together towards a common goal of success for the school, the teacher, and the student. In order to achieve our success we must foster understanding between each other, partnerships with our community, and remain viable as a school. This will be used to create an independent student who is self-assured and prepared for solving life's problems and securing life's opportunities.
- We, as students and staff, would like to be heard and have the ability to represent our goals on effective education and communication. We want to have a voice in the final decision by providing solid facts and feelings. This is our vision.

Regarding both of these projects, one an aggregate of small rural towns and the other inner-city urban, there are key commonalities that promote success.

The idea of making a commitment to the vision of involving students with real school and life problems had to come from key decision makers. Then, key adult champions needed to support the student efforts with both human and technical resources. The students had to make a commitment to take on the challenges and experiment with new skills and behaviors, as well as continue to sustain their motivation over a period of time. The point at which many projects fail is when continuous support of the initiative is needed. With adequate support, the initiative will eventually become embedded in the organization's culture. There is no easy answer. It takes hard work and involvement of all the stakeholders, even though it may begin with a small core group. Over the years, it has been found that inviting students to be partners in the process can catalyze a cultural impact quickly. Next, a planned strategy of ongoing internal and external support, assessment, and interventions is necessary to build a true, lasting change.

As for the common threads in creating the visions, students were trusted to come up with key concepts and, with an adult facilitator, to mold these concepts into a powerful statement. Every vision is inspiring and dares to suggest bold new horizons. There is an energizing and freeing element of being willing to create bold visions. On one hand, it can be challenging and risky, and/or it can be just what people need to move them to the next level of transforming themselves and their school community. In many cases, the student visions have served the purpose of raising the adult stakeholders' visions to new meaning and relevancy.

3

Building a Schoolwide Culture for Self-Esteem

Almost all of the literature suggests that the most effective strategies have to do with treating students as capable persons, capitalizing on their knowledge and interests, and involving them in determining goals and methods of learning.

—B. Levin (1994, p. 760)

How we talk to ourselves affects our self-esteem. If we say "I can do it," we have different thoughts and feelings than we do if we say "I can't." Similarly, saying "I know who I am and I know where I am going" creates a much different experience than does saying "I'm lost." To maximize and extend the personal powers of self-esteem, it is a necessity that self-talk is *respectful*. Self-talk should reinforce feelings of competence and a knowledge of personal abilities and strengths. It should emphasize a self-awareness and a desire for continuous improvement. It is always best to be willing to take positive risks and move outside normal comfort zones. Team members need to see that they can communicate their ideas and needs to others and that they are caring, loving, compassionate human beings. When each person recognizes these personal strengths, the ability to put forth the best possible efforts in the pursuit of excellence is enhanced. All of this self-talk is interconnected in one continuous flow, as in a circle: Competence, *Identity*, *Risk-taking*, Communication, *Loving*, and *Excellence*. The center point of the circle is equal distance from all points on

Think of self-esteem as a CIRCLE. A circle is complete.
It is the symbol for wholeness.

"C" COMPETENCE: I can do. It is a sense of power from
having the resources and capability to influence the
circumstances of our lives.

"I" IDENTITY: We know who we are and are capable of
acknowledging and respecting the qualities that make us
special.

"R" RISK-TAKER: Have the confidence to explore the
territories and experience new challenges.

"C" COMMUNICATION: The ability to express one's
ideas and relate to people of varied backgrounds.

"L" LOVING: Able to love one's self and to love others
for who they are.

"E" EXCELLENCE: They put forth their best efforts in
whatever they do. They are in touch with quality and
doing things right for the first time.

All are interconnected in one continuous flow, as is a
circle. The center point of the circle is equal distance from
all sides of the circle. It is the point of perfect balance, the
point of SELF-ESTEEM.

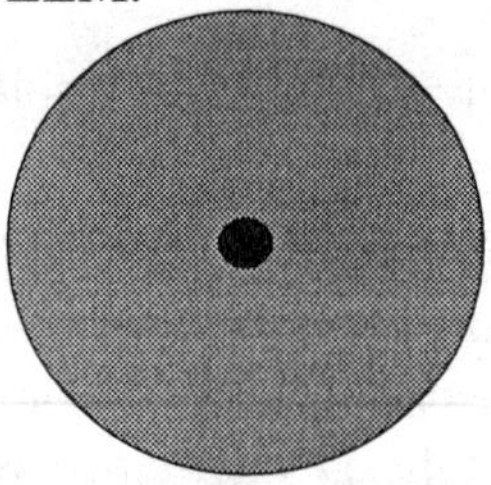

Figure 3.1. Self-esteem.

the circle. It is the point of perfect balance, the point of self-esteem (see
Figure 3.1).

Each person is a complex organism composed of many known and
unknown features. Science is continuously exploring the makeup of
humans in order to gain a greater understanding and appreciation for
how they operate and function. This is true whether the discussion
concerns human physiology or psychology. Through personal growth
and development, people find that there are secrets about themselves

that others have not yet discovered. There are also secrets that people are aware of but keep hidden from others. In addition, there are pieces of information that no one is aware of and that can be revealed on some future date. Each human being goes through life on a constant journey of awakening. The more one *learns* about one's self, personal abilities, and relationships to a larger world, the more opportunities a person has to blossom into an enlightened adult.

Personal enlightenment closely parallels the rebirth that medieval Europeans experienced during the Renaissance. So much of what the world was about lay hidden from most people through the efforts of some not-so-wise rulers and leaders of those dark ages. The enlightenment occurred when a few clerics began to question conventional wisdom and discovered that what was passed off as truth had no foundation in what was accepted as the absolute source of truth, the Bible. As efforts to refocus human existence now create a new rebirth for society, it is equally important to realize that each person is more than what appearances suggest. There must be an elevation to a new sense of personal *honesty*.

The JoHari Window, which is shown below (Figure 3.2), gives insight into four dimensions of self-awareness. The OPEN window is personal knowledge to which others have been given access. The BLIND window is what others know about a person that that person has not yet discovered. The HIDDEN window is personal knowledge that an individual chooses not to reveal to others. The MYSTERY window is unknown to all and is an area from which come constant revelations about a person's life, abilities, skills, and desires. An ideal to work toward is an ever-expanding OPEN window with an ever-shrinking MYSTERY window. Through self-discovery, personal mastery is obtained. The very essence of education is to lead out from within what is already known though not yet discovered: "educo."

As a result of self-discovery, personal strengths are magnified and weaknesses diminished. By drawing on an inner strength, positive self-worth grows, and quality and productivity increase. As individuals become more aware of effective and ineffective behaviors, and as they compare these behaviors to personal values, those ideas of right and wrong, people grow as contributing members of a healing society and community. This growth has a snowballing effect. Thus, the more the MYSTERY window is revealed, the more powerful the growth in the ability to relate to the world will be. With this power comes an ability to achieve worthy goals and promote personal mastery. In turn, there is a greater feeling of self-worth, and this encourages personal journeys of self-discovery and revelation of the inner existence. This

	Known to Me	Not Known to Me
Known to Others	OPEN	BLIND
Not Known to Others	HIDDEN	MYSTERY

Figure 3.2. JoHari Window.

allows the further revelation of core values and principles. This creates greater power and enhanced abilities to produce worthy outcomes. As value-adding tasks are accomplished, self-esteem spirals upward. Team members find themselves more able to make extraordinary contributions to their community and society as a whole.

If we are to determine one significant reason for helping every student find a more positive sense of self-worth, we believe it would be the manifold return to society from people who feel and think well of themselves. To use an often-cited quotation, "Love your neighbor as you love yourself." It is difficult to truly think well of and wish well for others when you think only ill thoughts of yourself. Before the ills of society can be healed, individual ills must be healed. The people, who are the basic composition of any society, are the point where improvement begins. Societal healing begins one person at a time and spreads geometrically as each healed person touches the lives of others. Another appropriate biblical quote is, "Remove the plank from your own eye before you remove the speck from someone else's eye." As long as the belittlement of even one person is tolerated, whether inflicted by others or self, heathy, whole communities will not exist. *Respect* for everyone and everything is crucial to feeling good about oneself.

If positive self-esteem is built on an individual basis, schools can progress to the point where groups of students can experience a sense of positive self-worth. As students with a strong sense of self-worth combine into caring, supportive, positive, *learning* communities, those learning communities can assemble into empathic, caring, healthy neighborhoods, cities, counties, states, and nations, and eventually, into a caring, loving, healthy world. The attitude that results will move schools forward on a journey that will start with a single step. Just one student, teacher, or parent who is dedicated to passing the energy and respect on to another can start the ball rolling. The service done will be that of creating an environment in which honest self-esteem is not a limited commodity but a geometrically expanding principle. The more one helps another person discover a positive self, the more positive self-esteem that person will possess. It is for this reason that we emphasize that quality leadership is *leadership of service*. The more we teach students to help others, the more ingenious they will become in helping themselves and others, and the more passion they will have for the Quality School transformation.

It is important to qualify this entire discussion of self-esteem. There are many people in our society who have advocated the development of self-esteem on false pretenses. Self-esteem without the quality works to support it is a hollow experience and will, more than likely, result in a more negative self-concept than ever before. It is critical that schools help children in school, at home, and in the community to learn the behaviors that lead to quality performance. As young people achieve and receive recognition for their ever-improving quality of performance, the self-worth that results will be lasting and self-perpetuating. It is critical that schools do not create a mythical self-esteem built upon a foundation of "feeling good." True self-esteem is grounded in having a positive attitude that reflects itself through self-respect and positive actions. Conversely, positive actions and the achievements those actions bring tend to help promote positive self-esteem. At the same time, it is very important to realize that no one will be successful 100% of the time. Therefore, along with the promotion of self-esteem generated by accomplishment, it is equally important that failure be destigmatized. Making mistakes is not a sin, but failing to learn from mistakes will impede long-term growth and development.

There is a great deal of accuracy in some of the objections voiced concerning some of the activities in the "self-esteem movement." Self-esteem for the glorification of the inner self that is not tied to a greater good is not a lasting self-esteem. Too often, it can turn into self-indulgence and into hedonistic pleasure seeking, devoid of any socially redeeming value. For self-esteem to have any positive value for the person, it must be related to the attainment of worthwhile goals. The continuous improvement of self and the organization are such goals. Although this discussion has focused on continuous improvement, it is important to realize that perfection is not possible. The pursuit of excellence is not the pursuit of perfection. Each successful effort toward continuous improvement will provide the framework for improved self-esteem. Another way to say this is that self-esteem is the memory of past successes.

Although self-esteem is an individual phenomenon, it does not exist separate from relationships to other people. It is also proper to note that the chance for students to achieve their goals can be dramatically enhanced when students learn to work as part of a team. It may be impossible for a person to move a 3,000-pound rock, and this could lead to that person feeling week and inadequate. A team effort, however, might result in moving that same rock, and this might help each person feel as if he or she has a certain amount of strength and control. Therefore, one very important tool in the process of building self-esteem is learning how to be an effective team member.

Much of what we have done with our Quality Student Leadership (QSL) workshops has focused on helping students take charge of their own lives and make a difference in their schools. In some of these cases, profound changes in both schools and students have occurred. Specifically, by empowering students to create a culture for continuous quality improvements, even the most at-risk populations begin to change their outlook on school. We have identified some specific programs and outcomes that demonstrate the impact of achievement on student self-esteem development.

Applications

Leadership for Challenged Students

For the very first time, challenged students from across the state of Iowa were invited to the "Student At-Risk Conference: Personal and Social Development for Challenged Students." The event is sponsored annually by the Iowa Department of Education, Iowa State Education Association, and the Drake University School of Education. The high school students were selected by their school districts as being challenged youth who nevertheless had leadership potential. It was a widely diverse mix of personalities, from withdrawn to rebellious to outgoing.

We were invited to work with these students using our QSL training. The purposes of this $1^{1}/_{2}$-day session were to (a) increase student involvement in the conference, and (b) get their input on strategies to assist challenged students in becoming successful. The format was to go through the QSL processes of self-esteem and team-work building, leadership development, and action planning. Next, the students were to put their new skills into action by creating a presentation for adult conference participants.

Quality Student Leadership Agenda

Day 1
   I. Overview
  II. Guidelines
 III. Commitment
  IV. Vision
   V. Paradigms (old and new)
  VI. Brainstorming in new paradigm
 VII. Student discussion: How to prepare staff/student team
      action in their individual schools
      a. How do students see it occurring?
      b. Barriers to new paradigm?
      c. How to get real action planning?
VIII. Closing

Day 2
   I. Student leadership video and discussion
  II. Preparation for student presentation to entire conference
      a. Clarify roles and content of report out
         1. Key student leaders
         2. Break into teams with other students and define roles
         3. Rehearse agenda
            Introduction
            Risk-taking: beyond comfort zones
            Team goals
            Old/new paradigms
            Student skit
            Action plans: What we are going to do with the
               information we learned
            Student leadership vision
            Q & A
            Wrap-up: Commitment from the adults to use the new
               paradigms of these students in their own school
               districts
 III. Students invite staff advisors to dialogue
      a. Staff shares their vision of student leadership and their
         commitment to support
      b. Students go through a rehearsal of their presentation to
         conference and staff critiques
  IV. Written evaluations and close
   V. Presentation by students to conference participants

One aspect of the QSL process that students have come to particularly enjoy is the Old Paradigm-New Paradigm activity. In this activity, students learn about the concept of paradigms and how those paradigms govern the way people respond to problems they face. Students can be asked to solve a problem that requires them to look beyond the box to find a solution. Once they get the idea of how paradigms can limit our ability to use our ingenuity to solve problems, they are frequently very capable of seeing their relationship with adults in a new light. The following lists were generated by students after the students went through a brief lesson on paradigms and their impact on critical and creative thinking.

Old Paradigms of How Adults View Students

Students don't know how to take care of own lives!
Not interested in anything but selves
Know it alls
Unfocused—just have fun
Don't know what talking about
Irresponsible
"When I was your age . . ."
Kids try to excuse what they do
Students have no right to question their teachers
Too immature to make decisions
"Because I said so!"
Our feelings don't count
Students thinking that not being successful in school means
    failure as a person

New Paradigms of How Adults Can View Students

Our opinions count
To earn respect you have to learn respect
Students have good ideas
Youth can invigorate
Really concerned about what happens
We do have feelings
We can make our own decisions
If we get ourselves into something, we can get ourselves out!
Teachers listen to students and help them out
Look deeper into who students are and how they feel

Don't label—I'm unique!
Together we can make this work
Get to know each other
Look inside the person
More student involvement in school

During the Iowa At-Risk Conference, the students used their collective skills to create a vision that could be used by any group of students at any school. This vision echoes the sentiments of youth and gives great hope for the future of our country. One thing is certain. Too many people in this country are far too pessimistic about the future. If we are not mistaken, each succeeding generation has been thought to be the most irresponsible and least prepared of all. Look at the vision developed by this group of at-risk high school students from all over the state, and then tell the world who is really at risk.

Student Leadership Vision

We believe that we can make a difference, as a team, through cooperation, determination, initiative, organization, and opportunity. We can use our leadership to accomplish our goal to change student leadership roles and attitudes. By working together, building each other up, and utilizing our individual strengths, we can accomplish our realistic goals and say—WE DID SOMETHING!

After completing the workshop, participants had several things to say about their experience. We believe that these comments send a message to the adults who are running the schools. If we unleash the power and ability to learn that exists within each of our students, there will be a reawakening in America. Trust begets trust, and power begets power. For our schools to become quality learning environments, we need only listen to our students to find out how. Pay attention to these comments from the at-risk students at this Iowa Conference.

"I learned about ways I could help myself, other students, and my school."

"The workshop was wonderful, it could change the U.S. nationally."

"To be more confident and feel better about myself."

"I learned not to judge people before I know them. Also, people are better than I think."

"To not worry what others think when I speak."

"There are a lot of students who are trying to be like others and need to learn to be themselves."

"It's all right to speak up."

"I learned how to work with a group."

"We need more caring adults to listen to us."

"I learned that students can make a difference in how their schools are run, and how to go about making those changes."

"I learned that I can make a difference in student's [sic] roles."

"I learned how to take risks."

"To be able to stand up for myself and take part."

The following year, we worked with challenged middle school students from Iowa. These middle school students focused on ways that they could take what they learned back to their own schools and begin to make a difference. Some of the action plans that these students brought back to their schools were the following:

1. Develop a student leadership group at each school.
2. Design an inservice for the whole school about the issues of harassment and violence.
3. Create a student mentorship program to assist younger students in learning appropriate behavior and social skills.

These middle-school students also created their own vision for their schools.

Student Leadership Vision Statement

WE THE LEADERS OF THE FUTURE DO HEREBY DECLARE THAT WE EXPECT AND WILL GIVE MUTUAL RESPECT.

WE ALSO DECLARE THAT WE ARE CAPABLE OF BEING RESPONSIBLE BY SHOWING LEADERSHIP AND BEING A GOOD ROLE MODEL IN SCHOOL AND AT HOME.

WE WANT TO BE RECOGNIZED AS PEOPLE OF THE 21ST CENTURY RATHER THAN CHILDREN OF THE 50's, 60's, AND 70's.

AS STUDENTS, WE WOULD LIKE TO PARTICIPATE IN EDUCATIONAL DECISIONS THAT AFFECT US DIRECTLY.

WE WOULD LIKE TO PARTICIPATE IN MORE ALTERNA-
TIVE AND MORE FUN WAYS OF LEARNING.

In conclusion, the outputs from both the middle and high school "challenged students" demonstrate a marked focus in declaring their readiness to be part of the solution, not the problem. What is looked for is the "educo" of education—to lead out from *within* a student's own innate wisdom. A vital part of the process is that facilitators provide the structure, content, and facilitation skills, and the students provide the "creative spark." This you can see from all the above outcomes: visions, paradigms, action plans, and evaluations.

We would like to change the idea from "challenged students" to "challenging students" to be the best they can be. Every person, whether young or old, thrives on looking to wider horizons where they are learning and growing. *We need to challenge our young people to fulfill their dreams!*

One of the most difficult populations to redirect is that of young people who have already found their way into the criminal justice system. Already hardened by experiences no child should have to endure, these youths often try to minimize their personal responsibility for the lives they now lead. Through the QSL process, these young people are given the opportunity to begin building a positive sense of self that stems from planning to take actions that can lead to a better life. Self-esteem is difficult to build when a 15-year-old's only contact with others is through the lock-ups at the juvenile detention center. Yet progress can be made when these youths are treated with dignity and respect and when they are taught how to take personal responsibility for their experiences in life.

In one workshop conducted with youth at a juvenile detention center, a step was taken to help heal the wounds and start building a foundation that will allow the youths to take on constructive roles in their communities. Their comments are included in the following section.

Inner-City Juvenile Detention Center for Youth

A unique half-day workshop was completed for 15 adolescents who were a mix of black and Hispanic youth. They were in the center by court order for numerous crimes. Their length of stay varied from 30 days to several years. One staff member attended the program.

The theme of the session was "Success." When we asked the youth to define success, we heard definitions such as "car," "money," "women," and so on. You could see the youth were not used to really communicating in a group. As part of our ground rules, the staff person had to participate as well.

We then discussed the idea of success being an inner experience rather than an external object. For example, when you want money or a car, what *experiences* are you really looking for? Some of the answers were freedom, security, peace, and joy. As we began to delve deeper into their true needs, you could see this awareness making an impact on them.

Next, we challenged the participants to come up with an affirmation using two to three key words that represented the experiences they wanted in their lives, such as "I want more freedom and joy in my life!" The next risk was to have each person stand up and state his affirmation in such a way that every person there understood it. It was essential that everyone recognize that each affirmation arose from a place of conviction, belief, and internal power. Each person could not sit down until everyone agreed that each person's affirmation was internalized as a powerful tool for transformation. As you can imagine, this process brought up a lot of feelings, from anger to frustration and from fear to laughter. What we observed was that the group did not allow any fellow youth to slide. They held each person to a high standard of accountability. This was also done for the staff person.

The outcome was nothing short of amazing. You could sense the newfound esteem and confidence, individually and collectively. They had reached deep down inside themselves and had confronted the old beliefs with new beliefs of purpose and success. They had not only received the support of the group, but they had given support! Supporting others is a true sign of leadership and emerging maturity. The staff person opened up his own learning about who these young men are and what they are capable of doing.

Now, as these young men lined up in their customary way to go back to their "jails," you could see that they had begun to outgrow this cultural norm. A seed had been sown, and it was now up to them to keep it growing. As is the case in some projects, the opportunity does not always exist to have long-term, ongoing contact with the youth. That is always the ideal. However, when there are only short-term interventions available, it is critical to do the absolute best to stimulate and activate a newfound esteem, commitment, and attitude that will serve the youth in their next growth steps. As you will see from the student comments below, this has certainly been encouraged.

Quality Student Leadership Workshop Evaluations for Juvenile Detention Center
(Note: individual ratings were given with 1 = low and 10 = high)

Staff Member Comments and His Rating:

I have learned that these boys can work together. I have been here for some while and to get these boys to cooperate with each other is amazing. These boys showed me that they are more intelligent than people tend to think. (Rating = 10)

Youth Comments and Their Ratings:

- Today I learned more than I can imagine. I would like to describe in detail the numerous ways I was helped, but unfortunately I can go on forever, and I will go on forever, knowing I have learned something that will better myself. (Rating = Worth more than 10)
- I learned that people care about me and that I can do more things with help from my friends. (Rating = 9)
- I learned to go for the gold and to be helpful to other people and show people the right way to go in life and to stay on the right path. (Rating = 8)
- Today I learned a good point in being more successful. I learned to keep trying when I feel like giving up. (Rating = 8)
- Today I learned how to be successful and that all people can change to do right after they do wrong. (Rating = 9)
- I learned to be more open but sometimes when you're too open, some people take kindness for weakness. I want to contemplate, in other words think about how this has helped me. (Rating = 8)
- I learned about myself. I have to be open and straighten out my life and to share my feelings with everyone and help other people in life that need help and I hope I could be a nice person like you. Thanks for helping with my feelings. (Rating = 10)

The average rating of the total group was 8.9.

These student evaluations again show what can be accomplished in a very short time if one uses the appropriate teaching and learning strategies. Please note the staff person's observations. He experienced a whole new way of working with these youth and saw that "they are more intelligent than people tend to think." Our hypothesis is that this is true with most of our challenged young people. They are intelligent, but this intelligence may be different from what we have come to expect. It may not be the typical academic intelligence, but one that demonstrates other "multiple intelligences." We will attempt to continue to weave into our book's theme of "empowering students to transform schools" this essential educational concept. Empowering students means not only involving them as leaders, but involving them as learners who are active and dynamic partners in our school communities. Only then will we begin the journey of a true community of learners.

4

Team Building and Organization
With Students

The organizations that will truly excel in the future will be the organizations that discover how to tap people's commitment and capacity to learn at all levels in an organization. Learning organizations are possible because, deep down, we are all learners. An organization's commitment to and capacity for learning can be no greater than that of its members.

At the heart of learning organizations is a shift of mind—from seeing ourselves as separate from the world to connected to the world. . . . It [the learning organization] is a place where people are continually discovering how they create their reality. . . . Real learning gets to the heart of what it means to be human. Through learning we re-create ourselves.

—Peter Senge (1990, p. 78)

A good portion of the literature that discusses educational needs for future employment focuses on teamwork. Nationally, numerous state Employability Skills Task Forces have created entire sections for student portfolio programs that center on teamwork skills. If the concept of Total Quality is viewed as an approach to life (personal or organizational), it is quickly recognized that each person is imperfect. Furthermore, it is an essential principle of quality that continuous improvement efforts should draw our organizational performance closer to a constantly improving standard of excellence. To accomplish this, it is imperative that the importance of teamwork be emphasized.

In recent years, the concepts of cooperative learning and content mastery have received some very bad reviews from more conservative segments of our population. A more careful review of the nature of American society might reveal that the placement of self over the needs of the team led to some of the most stunning national setbacks. Throughout the late 1970s and into the 1980s, American economic power slipped. Perhaps this was because we did not act as a united nation in the highly competitive global market. Our team has lacked focus and clarity of mission. To regain preeminence in global affairs, the American people must learn how to cooperate for the common good. As the United States moves toward the 21st century, the progress we make may relate to the teamwork movement that now permeates most successful corporations.

During World War II, the nation saw a unanimity of purpose and a clear and focused mission. Possibly more than at any other time in history, the American people rallied around those ideals. An overwhelming majority of the American populace got behind its leaders and charged onward toward a greater good. Once again, America is faced with a serious situation. This time, however, the enemy is not fighting with weapons of physical destruction. The enemy is fighting with the weapons of fear, divisiveness, prejudice, and ignorance. Once again, there is a need to create a clear and focused mission for the country. The vision must be toward the future, and it must include a renewed ability to work as a team.

As the best run businesses and industries begin to regain some of the economic power that seemed to be waning through the 1970s and 1980s, schools can look to them for some key success factors. Highly successful companies, such as 3M, Proctor and Gamble, W. L. Gore & Associates, and Borg-Warner, regard their employees as part of their corporate team, no matter what their position within the organization. If high-quality products are to be produced, then everyone must contribute to the process. Just as the concept of self-esteem is important to the individual, "team esteem" is important to an organization. Successful businesses understand that teams that work together create successes that lead to a feeling of worth and value in the organization.

Many schools have now accepted the example set by quality-minded businesses. One of these schools is Sturgis High School, in Sturgis, Michigan. Beginning in 1990, this innovative high school has created teams that consist of faculty, community, and students. Students have made a major contribution to the changes that the school has experienced. For the past 6 years, students have worked hand in hand with staff and community members toward the improvement of

1. Communication skills and practice
2. Critical thinking skills and problem solving
3. Sense of belonging
4. Acceptance of cultural diversity
5. Personal responsibility

As a result of student participation on these teams, some dramatic changes in the school have taken place. Most notable of these changes is the large number of student-designed, student-driven activities in which nearly 80% of the student body participates. Students have created a Cultural Unity Club, a Youth Advisory Council, a Peer Tutoring Program, the Quality Student Leadership Team, and several other organizations and programs designed to help focus the student body on quality improvements for the entire school.

To get students involved is truly not a difficult process. It does, however, take a commitment and a champion. It would be nice if the commitment came from school administration and the champion was a student activities advisor, but that is not necessary. Like so many other changes in our society, these changes do not have to start on a grand scale. In fact, they are generally much more successful if they start out small, demonstrate a significant change, and then gain support and steam from there. In the Sturgis High School example, mentioned above, it all began with a core of 40 students and one adult. From that, it has grown to more than 600 students and more than 100 adults.

The initial step begins with a dream and a champion. That dream can be the dream of the champion, or it can be someone else's dream. It is essential, however, that the champion adopt that dream as a vision for the future and then act in a way that promotes that vision to others. Again, in the Sturgis example, the champion's vision was shared with a core of students who became infected with a belief that they could make a difference. Within 2 years, this team of students was participating in quality improvement activities that began to make significant changes in practice and procedure for the high school. Those changes have opened floodgates that have substantially altered the culture of the high school. The by-products of those changes have been a dramatic reduction in discipline problems, an increase in student attendance rates, and a steady rise in test scores (see Figures 4.1 to 4.4).

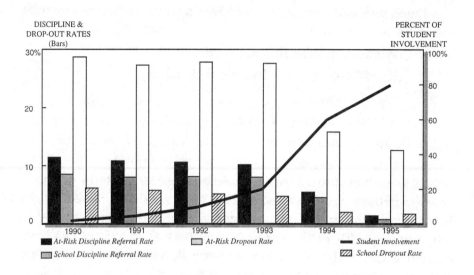

Figure 4.1. Sturgis High School improvement data.

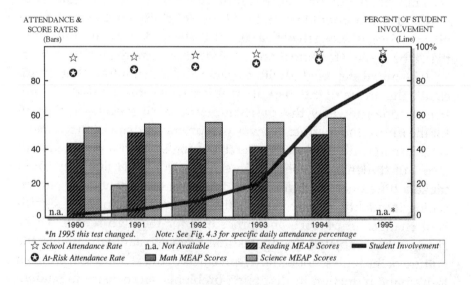

Figure 4.2. Sturgis High School improvement data.

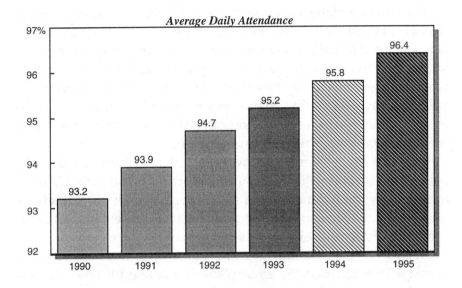

Figure 4.3. Sturgis High School improvement data.

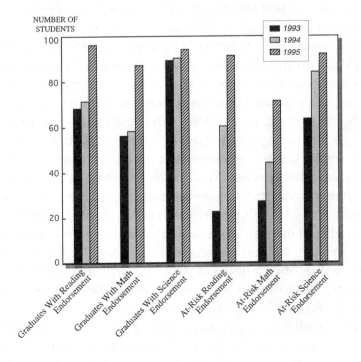

Figure 4.4. Sturgis High School improvement data.

Characteristics of Effective Teams

Perhaps one of the most difficult tasks we have in today's schools is getting our youth to truly work as teams. We have been a country of rugged individualists, and our schools have reinforced the concept of working individually. In fact, we punish students for cheating when, in many instances, these same acts would be considered to be a collaborative, team effort in businesses. Indeed, we want our youth to claim as their own only the work that they have done, but we do need to promote collaboration and teamwork.

How do we get students to work in teams? The answer is really quite simple, but it will take time and effort. To begin with, we need to remember the full meaning of the concept of leadership. Students must learn the 10 lessons of leadership that were presented in Chapter 1 and then apply those lessons within the context of a team.

Teams are interdependent units, within which, members value *learning*. They focus on the accomplishment of specific tasks that are geared toward meeting the goals of the organization. To achieve the highest quality outcomes possible requires that team members use the concepts of continuous improvement. As team members take a look at how they are doing, they are always looking for a better and more effective and efficient way to get the job done. This keeps learning at the forefront for the team at all times.

It is also important to remember that the dynamics of a good team are such that team members do whatever it takes to keep relationships within the team on a positive plane. A key to maintaining this team relationship is *empathy*. When team members think of how others will feel when they speak or take action, they make sure they treat others with dignity and respect. As teams go through natural progressions of development, it is not uncommon for team members to struggle with the empathy concept. In initial stages, there is usually an air of unfamiliarity, some standoffishness, and a general mistrust. This state can ease into a competitive relationship that frequently threatens the functionality of the team. Eventually, the team will move into a more mature working relationship and settle into the interdependent, inter-relating group of individuals that coalesces into a team. This team development process can be shortened when team members keep the goal and principle of empathy in mind.

Team excellence is dependent upon an *attitude* of excellence. Teams that focus on just doing good enough never progress to a level of true excellence. The excellence attitude requires team members to concentrate on quality and thus to be ever vigilant of ways to improve the quality of the team's work. This attitude promotes the constant study and evaluation of both process and product. It requires that team members focus on their mission and determine whether their actions are truly leading them toward their mission. In the life of an excellent team, attitude is everything.

This attitude of excellence allows team members to become singularly *dedicated* to the accomplishment of team goals. As individual members make the 100% commitment required for true quality, they lose their individualness without losing their individuality. A "team-think" arises and creates a synergy that allows the team to go beyond the collective potential of a group of individuals. Together, a group of dedicated team members accomplishes more than any group of separate individuals could ever hope to achieve. Together, everyone achieves more.

Teams have an *energy* that permeates the organization. Members infuse energy into one another and are careful not to use the language that saps a team of the energy needed to make the desired progress. Even when operating for long hours with very few breaks, excellent teams synergize in a way that keeps the energy level high. When things begin to sag, someone will take the leadership role and pump new life and energy into the system. There is a continual give-and-take within the team, and a new energizer will arise when it becomes obvious that a boost of energy is needed.

Quality team members have the highest level of *respect* for one another. It is recognized that each member of the team brings unique gifts and talents to the task at hand. If a goal is to be achieved, it is essential that team members work together toward its accomplishment. Working together requires that team members have the highest respect for each other and the skills others bring to the process. This respect recognizes the value of diversity of backgrounds and thought. New and creative ideas are the product of welcoming variations on old themes. Teams must respect divergent thinking if members are expected to take the risks necessary to suggest unique and original solutions to difficult problems faced by the team.

The purpose of the team is to bring the organization closer to the achievement of its mission. In this way, the team provides an important *service*. For the team to be viable, the service it provides must be critical to the structure and function of the organization. Teams will not function as teams for very long if they believe that their efforts are not directed toward goals that will truly enhance the existence, function, and operation of the organization. Effective teams realize that there is significance to the service they provide to the organization.

Through *honest* interactions, team members learn to become inter-dependent. When team members learn to be honest with themselves and other members of the team, a level of trust results that allows the team to become more efficient and effective in its endeavors. To be honest with others, team members must first be open and honest with themselves with respect to motive and attitude about the team. False pretense will fester within the team and soon be recognized as a sore spot that stifles productivity and the achievement of valued goals for the organization. The ultimate service to the organization for which the team was formed will be difficult to achieve if an appropriate level of honesty is not maintained.

Using *ingenuity*, creative solutions to old teamwork obstacles are discovered. A team synergy results that provides an opportunity for the entire organization to progress. Effective teams understand that doing things the way they have always been done will most likely produce the same results the team or organization has always gotten. To break new ground and find new ways to operate carries an expec-tation for the ingenious. The team is open to the creativity that allows for new approaches, divergent thought, and critical analysis of all processes in an ongoing search for continuous quality improvements.

Finally, a *passionate* team has the drive to achieve extraordinary outcomes. Teams devoid of passion lack the spark and inspiration needed to persevere when the going gets difficult. By keeping the goal in mind and making a 100% commitment to that goal, the team brings the dream, which the goal represents, to reality. Passion is born from a total commitment to dreams that the entire team embraces as being essential to the organization. When teams dare to dream, amazing things happen.

If teams learn and accept the lessons of leadership, they take a giant step toward greater effectiveness. Never assume, however, that simply learning these lessons will produce harmonious team relation-ships. As is the case with all quality efforts, the acquisition of quality is not so much a procedure or a process as it is a way of life. Certainly, in teams as in life, not all endeavors will pan out. Quality teams, however, use their less effective experiences as learning laboratories that provide the knowledge that will help the team be more effective in future efforts.

> The successful organization has one major attribute that sets it apart from unsuccessful organizations: dynamic and effective leadership. (Hersey & Blanchard, 1977, p. 83)

What is often needed in organizations is more emphasis on team building where people are hired who complement rather than replicate a manager's style. (Hersey & Blanchard, 1977, p. 153)

Applications

Total Quality Student Involvement

Another school making a significant commitment to increasing student participation is Gage Park High School, Chicago, Illinois. This school was part of the Total Quality Management initiative at Northwestern University's J. L. Kellogg Graduate School of Management, which focused on a number of Chicago public schools. Each school had representatives who were the principal and two other staff members. As Gage Park High School embarked on the second year of its Total Quality School program, they adopted the Quality Student Leadership (QSL) and Quality Leadership principles (for adults) and process (Figure 4.5).

The principal's vision was to have students involved in the school's decision-making committees, along with faculty management teams. The purpose was to have faculty, students, and parents become cohesive units, working together, to strategically develop and implement an energetic, successful environment for learning and teaching. A student leadership training workshop was set up to give a core of students the leadership and team skills necessary to participate with the adult teams (Figure 4.6). The students used the Team Organization Worksheet to form and organize their team mission, goals, and strategies for addressing specific school improvement areas.

An important outcome of the student leadership training conducted at an inner-city high school was a set of recommendations to the faculty management teams. These recommendations have assisted the school in improving the overall quality of teacher-student interactions. Logically, one would hope that improved teacher-student relationships result in greater cooperation and improved instruction. Indeed, in many cases that have been studied, this is the end result. The following recommendations were produced by students in the inner-city high school mentioned above.

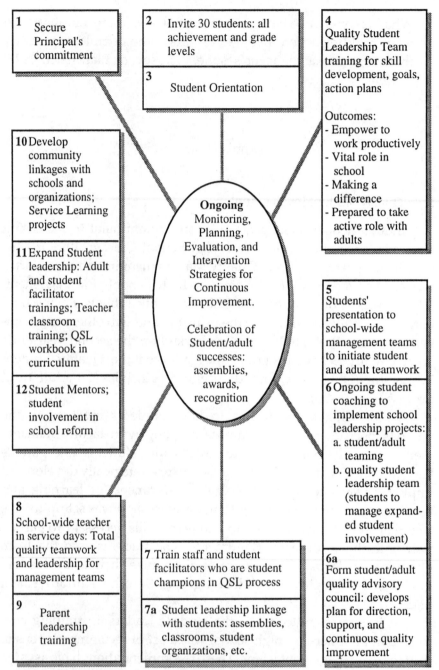

1 Secure Principal's commitment

2 Invite 30 students: all achievement and grade levels

3 Student Orientation

4 Quality Student Leadership Team training for skill development, goals, action plans

Outcomes:
- Empower to work productively
- Vital role in school
- Making a difference
- Prepared to take active role with adults

10 Develop community linkages with schools and organizations; Service Learning projects

11 Expand Student leadership: Adult and student facilitator trainings; Teacher classroom training; QSL workbook in curriculum

12 Student Mentors; student involvement in school reform

Ongoing Monitoring, Planning, Evaluation, and Intervention Strategies for Continuous Improvement.

Celebration of Student/adult successes: assemblies, awards, recognition

5 Students' presentation to school-wide management teams to initiate student and adult teamwork

6 Ongoing student coaching to implement school leadership projects:
   a. student/adult teaming
   b. quality student leadership team (students to manage expanded student involvement)

6a Form student/adult quality advisory council: develops plan for direction, support, and continuous quality improvement

8 School-wide teacher in service days: Total quality teamwork and leadership for management teams

9 Parent leadership training

7 Train staff and student facilitators who are student champions in QSL process

7a Student leadership linkage with students: assemblies, classrooms, student organizations, etc.

Figure 4.5. Master plan for student empowerment.
Note: Phase 1 = 1-6; future phases = 7-12.

STEP 1. TEAM IDENTIFICATION

1. Name of team: —————————————————————

2. School: ———————————————————————

STEP 2. MISSION: What is the team's mission?

———————————————————————————————

———————————————————————————————

———————————————————————————————

STEP 3. STRATEGIES: What are the team's strategies
for fulfilling its mission?

———————————————————————————————

———————————————————————————————

———————————————————————————————

———————————————————————————————

———————————————————————————————

———————————————————————————————

STEP 4. CUSTOMERS: For whom does the team
provide outputs?

———————————————————————————————

———————————————————————————————

———————————————————————————————

———————————————————————————————

Figure 4.6. Team organization worksheet.

STEP 5. OUTPUT/ASSIGNMENTS: What does this team provide its customers? or What are this team's assignments?

_____

_____

_____

_____

_____

STEP 6. MEMBERS: Who are the members of the team?

_____   _____

_____   _____

_____   _____

_____   _____

STEP 7. REPORTS: To whom will reports of the team's work be submitted?

_____   _____

_____   _____

_____   _____

_____   _____

STEP 8. SUB-GROUPS: What groups, committees or other sub-units are part of the team?

_____   _____

Figure 4.6. (Continued)

Quality Student Leadership Team Recommendations to the Faculty Management Teams

Teacher/Student Recognition

1. Students would like to have "more student input in recognition programs."
2. If [a student] and a teacher/faculty member have a disagreement and [the student] feels that the punishment given was unjust, then the student should be able to have some sort of court where both sides of the story are heard. If these problems are heard by a "judge" and a jury consisting of teachers and students randomly picked, students will be more likely to accept the decisions.

Behavior/Discipline/Safety/Security

1. Students would like more days when we have metal detectors.
2. There is a need for more security guards, including women guards.
3. Establish a three-strikes remedy. After three serious offenses, a student should forfeit his or her right to be in school.
4. Instead of suspending people, let them do work services (cleaning bathrooms, sweeping and mopping the halls, etc.). Use detentions, not suspensions.
5. Enforce that there is no gang activity around the school.

Crisis Intervention and Peer Mediation

Students also had some recommendations in the area of student-to-student interactions. As has been the case in many QSL workshops, students have had a profound desire to create a more peaceful and caring environment for schools. Although many adults believe that today's youths are more concerned about themselves than they are about others, the truth is that students want a good education in safe, secure, positive schools. Some of the ideas generated by students have been the following:

1. Hotlines: When personal problems become too great for an individual to bear, there should be someone available for the

troubled youth to call. Rather than resort to violence directed at self or others, a student could have a helpful conversation with someone who cares.

2. Peer cruising: Students who have learned how to deal with the difficulties of school and life in general could be used to move about the school and community to help those students who have not figured out how to handle difficult situations successfully.

3. Gang members: Talk with and about gang members and how they got out. Their stories can help inspire other students to make the move toward greater responsibility and help make a safer school.

4. Fund-raisers: Raise funds for people who are in money trouble. Money isn't everything, but students without money are too often looking for the wrong way to get the money they need to be successful in school.

5. Mentor program: Some students need positive, successful role models. There needs to be a natural connection with those people in the community who have made it. They can share their experiences with those who are having difficulty finding any reason for hope.

Student Recruitment

Successful programming requires good personnel. The QSL process is no different. Finding students who will work for the positive changes needed requires that the team have specific strategies for finding the best possible leaders. In this inner-city high school example, the core of leaders developed their expectations for students who would participate in the program and strategies for getting those students to be involved. It should be noted that strategies may vary depending upon the climate and culture of a particular school.

In one inner-city high school, it was determined that participants should be doing well academically. It was believed that having a solid work ethic would lead to positive academic experiences, and that those experiences would earn the respect of other students and the teaching staff. Without that respect, it would be difficult to make an impact on the school. Another important aspect was participation in extracurricular activities. It was believed that students who have already involved themselves in school are more willing to make the commitments necessary to make real progress. Although there was a desire to use extracurricular activities as a criterion for recruitment, it was also important to realize that there were other extracurricular activities besides athletics. Schools need to look at activities such as drama, music, and service organizations, as well as athletics.

To the credit of the student leaders selected in this project, they recognized the importance of keeping potential dropouts in school and getting those who left to come back. To increase the chances that students will remain in school and become involved in making the school a better place for students to learn, schools need good teachers and counselors who care about students and their world. It is not enough, however, just to have these good teachers and counselors. The word has to get out that all students are welcome, and the students need to feel that they are part of the school. In this particular high school, student leaders felt that the school should produce some quality flyers that could be sent to local families so that they would know how good the school really is.

Parental Involvement/Community Support

Once students have been brought back to the school by demonstrated excellence, a new job is created. That new job is keeping the students in school until they graduate. The students from this inner-city high school stated a firm belief that parents and community members are needed if a true incentive for graduation is to be created. If students do not see that the adults in the community value education, they will not be very apt to place much value on education themselves. Considering this idea, the students made the following suggestions:

1. Bring parents into the school to see what's going on.
2. Get more parents to be part of the school and involved in school activities.
3. Keep parents/community informed on school news (newsletter).
4. Inform the community about good news.
5. Train parents so that they can help with student problem mediation.

School Pride, Spirit, and Beautification

Students also looked for ways to increase the feeling of pride in the high school. As most educators know, many students feel little or no connection to the building that they call school. There are many reasons why this occurs, but we believe that one of the most important issues is a lack of fulfillment of the students' need for power and belonging. There is no ownership of the building and school grounds because those facilities do not help the students connect to their own personal world. At the same time, many of these students can easily express concern about the state of our natural environment. A group of inner-city students decided that the main reason many of their classmates did not show a concern for their school was because they had no part in the process of school.

To help students connect with the high school, these students (as with other groups of students in suburban and rural school districts) decided that a key would be to connect the school to some of the greater issues facing our world today. It was believed that involving students in activities that promoted positive outcomes for the community and environment would help to connect the students to the school and improve the school's position within the community. Some of the activities that students suggested were the following:

1. Start a recycling program: waste baskets for cans, paper, plastic, aluminum.
2. Put more murals in the hallways and classrooms.
3. Plant more trees on the school grounds.
4. Place garbage cans in the hallways.
5. Paint the lunchroom, ROTC room, and gym rooms.
6. Fix up the girls' locker room.
7. Exterminate rats and roaches—especially in lunchroom.
8. Provide a better variety in food—healthier and better quality.
9. Put plants in all classrooms or create a greenhouse in the hallway.

Extracurricular/Enrichment Programs

A key to getting students involved is to have activities in which students want to involve themselves. Therefore, it is critical that students have some input into the types of extracurricular activities offered within the school. Quality Student Leaders want their fellow students to get people involved in their school sports teams. They also want their students to be involved in the school clubs that already exist and to create new ones.

Once teams of students, staff, and parents have worked on the myriad problems faced by students in their everyday school experience, many programs would bring the tasks to closure. In the QSL process, we know that we are only halfway home. For any system to be of quality, there must be an evaluation and replanning stage. For students to add quality to their lives, they need to learn that every activity must have a quality assessment followed by planning for improvements. This continuous quality improvement concept is the cornerstone of the QSL process. It is the concept that allows the empowerment of students to transform schools into quality learning communities.

Continuing to use the inner-city high school model, the evaluation process has taken this form:

Quality Student Leadership Assessment of
Faculty Management Team Involvement

What Worked	*What Did Not Work*
Adults solicited the students' opinions and listened to students	Some of the students didn't get to pick team they were on
We have a better understanding of teachers and how to help them	Students should have own meetings, as well as adult meetings
Teachers see us as partners, not just kids	Didn't have other QSL teams to help with adult teams
Found out that teachers we didn't know or like were likable	Didn't have enough opportunity to put my ideas into action
Was able to meet more people and help school	QSL team and student council should work hand in hand and get more council trained
Teacher/student teams accomplished a number of projects and enjoyed seeing their efforts turn into tangible results	Didn't get along with some of the adults on my team
Liked being able to make a difference on the behalf of the student body and the school climate	Wasn't able to make all meetings
Teachers acting more respectful to [the student leaders] and other students as well	School needs to support student participation more:

1. Set standards resulting in a letter
2. Clear letter of support from principal
3. Talk to LSC about what want and need

The experiences we have had with so many students from all over the United States have taught us to listen to the wisdom of youth. After each QSL workshop, student participants are asked to provide input into how the experience can be made better. These students have done a great service for future participants by giving excellent recommendations for improvements to the process. Some of the more notable suggestions have been summarized in the following section.

Quality Student Leadership Training Improvements (from student leaders)

Set the following criteria for ongoing student participation

1. Keep track of attendance on teams.
2. Make grades a consideration, yet allow for diversity on teams.
3. Provide a time to meet after school and, on occasion, time to meet during school.
4. Choose participants who are open-minded.
5. Choose participants who are committed students who want to help their school and work together.
6. Remember that Quality Student Leaders need internal champions (teachers or administrators). Get a clear, specific commitment from champions to support student ideas and be part of the workshop. In most cases, the internal champions will be teachers or administrators who believe that students are a critical link to the creation of a positive culture for quality change within the school.

In the majority of situations, when creating a culture that allows for student involvement on quality improvement teams, the students will become actively involved in the processes that draw immediate and positive attention to the process. Many young people have a great need to be part of something. This need for belonging draws students into activities that tend to be highly visible. In some negative instances, this can lead to gang affiliations. When this need is directed toward the improvement of their school and community, the result will be a flurry of activities that positively promote the school, community, and the student involvement process. A typical set of actions taken by students following their inclusion into the realm of school improvements is listed below.

Student Leadership Actions to Promote Student Involvement

- Better PR sheet to involve students: Promotional sheet: list of students' vision things done by student leaders
- Article in school news
- Ads in school yearbook (school, business)
- QSL team T-shirts and banner group photo for yearbook

An important product of each school's QSL involvement process is the development of a team vision. When students begin to dream about the potential for their school, new energy and excitement appear. One of the inner-city high schools that has gone through the QSL student empowerment process is located in Chicago. These students created this vision.

Student Vision Statement

Our school is a school of excellence. We believe that the quality of our school nurtures the minds of our students. We often praise our students to give them the enthusiasm and self-esteem to achieve their goals. In order to meet our goals, we must have discipline and cooperation. We teach our students to be creative and use that creatively as a plan for success and that is our motto:

EXPECT *SUCCESS* AND NOTHING LESS!

Considering their participation and the vision they created, these students set some specific school improvement goals. These were the following:

1. Expand academy programs
2. Consider extended school day
3. Eliminate overcrowding
4. Need more audio video equipment
5. In classroom we would like teachers to be more open
   a. Listen to students' opinions about teaching
   b. Different teaching techniques—more interaction with students
   c. Control the "troublemakers"
   d. Connect learning to real world situations

6. An open door plan with the principal for students
7. Current student ideas and events shared by monthly news-letters
8. More classes on how to get into internet on computer

In summary, the student involvement project at this high school successfully affected the participants and the school's culture. Students who were labeled as low achieving and as having behavior problems became enthusiastic problem solvers and demonstrated the ability to challenge themselves and others in working on school improvement efforts. Various authentic assessment outcomes have been demonstrated through student planning, plan implementation, assessments of school function with respect to plans, restructuring of project ideas, and follow-up reflections. Figures 4.7 and 4.8 demonstrate how this system works. The action planning sheet in Figure 4.7 assisted students with a systematic guide to identifying goals and making them quantifiable and realistic. The idea is that the more specific the goals, the greater the chance for team success. The student vision and action-planning worksheet shown in Figure 4.8 provides a structure to help students work in small teams to create focused action plans for supporting their school's improvement efforts.

Both students and adults involved in this experience have observed powerful growth and personal advancement. One of the keys, which this chapter highlights, is team building and organization. Students come into these projects as individuals and leave possessing the skills needed to be effective team members. They were able to expand their horizons greatly by working with adults, as well as working independently of them. They experienced frustrations and failures as well as successes. This is certainly a key that can be applied in school and to future life situations.

Students were given the opportunity to be involved and to contribute to their own school's improvements. What an exciting and sometimes awesome responsibility. There is no replacement for this kind of experience. Real leadership in action working on real problems has made this experience a vital part of these students' lives, and it has also affected those adults who opened their minds and hearts to make a place for these young people.

1. Specific Goal: _____

_____

2. Measurable: Looking at goal and timeframe. Being able to
  say, "I accomplished . . ."

3. Achievable: Yes or No (if no, go back to #1 and reset goal)

4. Road map: Specific action steps
Action steps   Timeframe

1.	
2.	
3.	
4.	
5.	

5. Roadblocks   **Solutions**

1. _____

2. _____

3. _____

6. Resources: Who/What do I need for support of the plan?

1. _____

2. _____

3. _____

7. Reward: How do we celebrate our success/s?

_____

_____

_____

8. Timeframe: Specific dates starting or completed by (fill in #4)

Name—————————————Position/Role _____
Team Members' Names _____

Figure 4.7. S.M.A.R.T. action-planning sheet.

1. Write student leadership support *vision:*

Example: Our student leaders will be working as a leadership group and demonstrating leadership by working on a school improvement project/s. They will continuously report to the principal and teachers regarding their progress. The adults of the school will provide support and recognition as the students progress.

_____

_____

_____

4. Develop an action plan for *supporting* quality student leadership in your school.

Action step 1	How	When	Who
Action step 2			
Action step 3			

Additional Action Steps:

4. _____

_____

5. _____

_____

Figure 4.8.

5

Generating Creative Success

Planning for Action

There are many who are living far below their possibilities because they are continually handing over the individualities to others. Do you want to be a power in the world? Then be yourself. Be true to the highest within your Soul.

—Ralph Waldo Trine (quoted in Seldes, 1985, p. 451)

Planning for Action

The chain is no stronger than its weakest link. We have found a weak link, so what do we do? We have choices to examine, and the way we examine those choices and generate additional choices will require that we use creative thought. An old paradigm solution might be to remove the weak link and replace it with a new and, it is hoped, stronger link. A new paradigm might be to try to strengthen the present link. To take either course of action without using the creative energies of the entire team could be disastrous for the team. Indeed, there might be other options to consider.

Creative thinking is the practice of seeing things in new ways and envisioning unique possibilities. It is a skill we all have and one that can be developed through training and practice. Unfortunately, we often, unwittingly, stifle creativity through the means we use to educate children. If we are to develop powerful teamwork skills in today's youth, they must have the creative abilities to pose unique solutions to old problems and innovative solutions to new problems. Independently, these skills will be helpful, but collectively, as a team effort, these skills can become an awesome force for positive change.

In the March 1994 edition of the *Arithmetic Teacher*, Larry Buschman reports some interesting observations made in an elementary mathematics class. This teacher noted that student behaviors changed dramatically when they were not given sample solutions to problems. The most dramatic differences were the success rate at solving math problems, communication styles used, and the attitudes the students had about the means for solving posed problems.

In this article, Buschman notes that students were more successful at solving the math problems when they were not given solution examples. He believes this occurs because the students do not feel tied to one solution methodology and are open to divergent thinking. When solution examples are given, the success rate drops, which appears to result from students' attempts to apply the example, in the same format, to all posed problems. Buschman also notes that communication is open and supportive when no solution example is given, whereas it is much more closed and combative when examples are given. A major difference in student attitudes demonstrates our tendency to adhere to a plan even if it does not apply to the situation at hand. When no model solution is offered, we are left to our own creative powers to suggest solutions; evaluate the probability of success; test our hypotheses; readjust our efforts, if necessary; and then go about the business of solving the problem.

This concept of problem solving is much more consistent with Total Quality Management than is the model solution approach. A Total Quality approach asks us to examine examples of Total Quality Organizations not so that we can copy what they do but so we might gain an understanding of the systemic way in which the organization operates. It is the systems approach that is important, not the actual steps a Total Quality Organization takes to create its effective system. Creative thinking can be stifled by adhering too tightly to "a model of excellence."

Creative thinking is important to team thinking and planning because it often takes a creative new approach to go from current situations to an improved, highly desired state. Most often, we need to think of a number of ideas before we find one or more that will be useful to us in solving our problems. Indeed, at times, the solution possibilities we generate will create other problems. Thus, we want to examine as many possibilities as we can so that we can minimize the adverse side effects created by the solution we implement.

To increase our creative energy, it is necessary that we be open to a variety of possibilities and that we use divergent thinking skills. For some people, creativity can be somewhat uncomfortable. This often occurs because creative solutions can take us outside our perception of an orderly world. Creative thoughts can seem silly because they do not adhere to the rules as we have experienced them in the past. Those people who feel that they are not very creative need to be open and patient with their creative side, because it is from this unstructured thinking that new ideas are generated. In the past, many good ideas have been thought of as ridiculous by mainstream thinkers. In our own experiences, we recall many high school students who have brought something to a classroom only to be squashed by unresponsive adults. In one case, one student brought one of the first electron micrographs of a molecule to his chemistry teacher with great enthusiasm. That chemistry teacher laughed and told him it was a hoax. He told the student that it was impossible to photograph molecules. That student's father won a Nobel Prize for his advancements in electron micrography. It is too bad that that teacher was so limited in his vision and thus was stuck in a paradigm that limited his growth and development.

Stretching beyond our paradigmatic boundaries into new dimensions of thoughts and explanations of our world is the very basis of creative thought. This stretch significantly affects the quality of life in a learning organization and helps to establish an expectation for the continuous improvement of the processes that lead to the products of the organization. This, in turn, leads to the continuous improvement of outcomes and the organization as a whole. To make this stretch requires that participants be willing to take positive risks. Inherent with every risk is the potential for failure. Thus, it is essential that new ideas be implemented using a plan-do-study-act cycle (PDSA), and creative thinking teams must be free of the fear of ridicule and reprisal should the implementation of a creative idea not produce the desired outcome. Team members need to be supported in these situations. Through the study phase of the PDSA cycle, evaluation of the processes used should be restricted to structure and function issues rather than focusing on people, ideas, or thinking frames.

Experimentation is an important part of the creative thinking process. The identification of perceived problems and the suggestion of hypothetical solutions provides the opportunity for team members to risk beyond the realm of conventional wisdom. It was this freedom to risk that led Thomas Edison to the light bulb, Alexander Graham Bell to the telephone, and George Eastman to modern photography. An essential adjunct to these creative thoughts, however, is the critical analysis that follows the initial implementation of a new idea. This critical thinking allows us to study the effects of our creative endeavors.

Deming understood this concept and thus created his PDSA cycle. Improvement requires creative solutions to our problems. If we continue to apply the same solutions to recurrent problems, we will have the same level of success we have always experienced. In other words, if you keep on doing what you have always done, you will keep on getting what you have always gotten. Organizational improvement cannot occur without creativity, yet it is important to realize that creativity does not guarantee improvement. Each innovation must be evaluated for its effectiveness in achieving desired outcomes. Therefore, innovations need to be tested. Thus, we experiment. As is the case in the scientific world, the experiment is not done until we collect the data and evaluate that data to see if our hypothesis was correct. Does our innovation produce the outcomes we anticipated? If it does, are we sure it was the innovation, or are there some other factors involved that we have not considered? If we do not get what we were looking for, is there something in the design of our innovation that could be modified and thus change the outcome? It is fairly common knowledge that Edison modified his innovation hundreds of times until he finally reached a solution that adequately addressed his problem. Creative thinking requires patience.

At times, an organization may need a means for jump-starting the creative processes. Perhaps the most widely used technique is brainstorming. The purpose of brainstorming is to generate a large number of ideas. You can brainstorm approaches, alternative courses of action, causes, effects, options, results, probabilities, or anything else, and mix and match them as well. The purpose is to seek as many ideas as possible, not to evaluate the ideas for their chances for success. Judging ideas should be avoided until all ideas have been expressed because critical comments tend to corrupt and disrupt the creative process.

Here is an effective technique for quality brainstorming:

1. If possible, tell team members what will be brainstormed before the meeting, or at least give the team time to collect their thoughts before you start.
2. Take turns telling what your ideas are while someone records every idea.

3. Team members may also spontaneously share their ideas. It is often the case that hearing other members' ideas triggers creative ideas in our own minds. Thus, getting the ball rolling with a round-robin of ideas can generate a great deal of additional ideas.

4. The social atmosphere should be open. Playfulness and random thoughts should be encouraged. All ideas are recorded, regardless of how silly or impractical they may seem. These silly notions can stimulate other ideas that just might be the key to success.

5. Negative attitudes and remarks are not permitted.

6. After many ideas have been recorded, try to think of ways that ideas might be combined to form new ideas.

7. Experiment with models and drawings of any kind to change perspectives.

8. Relax and enjoy yourself. You are creating, which is one of the highest forms of human activity.

9. When the "well of ideas" runs dry, it is a good time to take a break or end the meeting. Team members should be given a copy of all brainstormed ideas and encouraged to think of more ideas and review the ideas before the next session.

At Sturgis High School in Sturgis, Michigan, the Quality Student Leadership (QSL) team used the brainstorming process to identify what were felt to be the major barriers to achieving its mission of creating a culture that promotes the philosophy that "All students can learn, and it's everybody's job to help that learning happen." Some of the barriers identified in that brainstorming activity were the following:

1. Low self-esteem
2. The lack of transitional activities for eighth graders as they move from the middle school to the high school
3. Past failures and the failure syndrome
4. A phenomenon the students called the "drag-down syndrome," which says "If I'm going to fail, I'm going to take some other kids with me"
5. Low achievement motivation
6. Negative parental attitudes
7. Lack of family support for learning
8. Lack of recognition for accomplishments

9. Lack of benchmarks for achievement and lack of authenticity in evaluation of students

10. Lack of positive role modeling for expected behaviors

Considering this list of barriers, the QSL team designed a mentoring program that would help to instill in new students a stronger belief in the school's mission. This mentoring program has been implemented and is helping to focus the vision and bring the mission to life.

Once a problem has been identified and proposals have been generated that might lead to a solution of that problem, a new phase of the decision-making, team development process comes into play. The next section of this chapter is devoted to the development and nurturing of the critical thinking skills that will be necessary if the best possible solutions are to be implemented into success-generating action plans.

Critical Thinking and the
Ethic of Continuous Improvement

The passing of the industrial era means the passing of the usefulness of standardization as an organizing educational principle. "What all literate citizens should know" will no longer be a major concern. It is not possible to predict exactly the knowledge base required of productive citizens in the global/service-oriented/ information age. It is also impossible to "cover" all the information in a human's lifetime. We can be sure, though, that all citizens will need to solve problems, to think creatively, and continue to learn. (Costa, 1989, p. vii)

One aspect of the thinking skills mentioned in this quotation is problem solving. To effectively solve problems, a person must be able to think critically about the possible solutions generated and thus evaluate potential outcomes of the actions taken. Critical thinking is the practice of examining statements and/or pieces of information in order to make decisions about their accuracy and usefulness. It is a skill we all possess and one that can be refined through training, practice, and the desire to improve. Critical thinking is an important skill for problem solving and planning, for both depend on evaluating facts, applying logic, and making decisions. Successful team building and development require that team members be effective problem solvers and proficient planners.

The need for quality decision making and problem solving in an organization often drives team members to seek one best way to use critical thinking skills. In reality, though, there is no one best way to think critically through one's observations and experiences. Critical thinking is a situational skill that must be applied in the manner most appropriate for the circumstances that exist at any given time. It is also essential that we realize that there may be more than one correct way to solve a problem, and that the most important criterion is the effectiveness and efficiency of the solution used.

The concept of maximum effectiveness and efficiency is a primary, driving force in most real-world situations. It is part of the natural world that pushes all living things toward a state of maximum conservation. Expend the minimum amount of resources possible to acquire the maximum output of product. All living systems adhere to this principle, and human organizations should make this paramount in their systems management schemes. To create a team that has the greatest opportunity to follow this natural law, it is important that all team members become excellent thinkers. Excellent thinkers all have the ability to analyze a situation critically and make wise decisions about how to best proceed. This does not mean that mistakes are not made, it simply means that fewer mistakes will occur when appropriate critical thinking skills are used prior to taking action.

To assist in the critical thinking process, there are some suggestions that can be most beneficial. A few of these are the following:

1. Test assumptions whenever it is possible. Facts can only be deduced from other facts. Primary sources of information, those who actually witnessed the event, are generally more credible than secondary sources. Eye witnesses, however, can sometimes be inaccurate in their perception of the details of an incident. It is important to review the biases and prejudices of a witness or observer, which might affect that person's perceptions. To simply accept as fact whatever is stated by an individual without scrutinizing those statements can lead to incorrect conclusions that, in turn, can detract from the effectiveness of decision making. Remember, if your premise is wrong, your conclusions will likely be wrong.

2. Avoid generalizations, particularly hasty ones or those based on few facts or observations. Although generalizations can

assist in understanding trends and tendencies, they can also result in a stilted or slanted view of a situation.

3. Be sensitive to the difference between facts and opinions. Facts can be proven and substantiated through additional observations or corroborating evidence. Opinions, regardless of how strongly they are held and sincerely expressed, cannot be proven. Within this context, it is important to further differentiate between opinion and bias. An informed decision maker will make decisions based on opinion that can be supported through a solid body of evidence. Even though the opinion cannot be proven as fact, it can be important when trying to solve complex problems. Biases, however, lack a solid supporting foundation and thus can negatively influence the quality of the decision to be made.

4. Patience is an important virtue in decision making and timing is critical. When adequate time permits, decision makers should gather all possible facts to assist in the process. When time is short, it is still important to gather as much information as possible before coming to a conclusion. Jumping to conclusions greatly detracts from the reliability of the decision-making effort and directly impacts the organizational climate. In today's organizational climate of shared decision making, teams of decision makers will collect information, share ideas and opinions, and come to a consensus when making decisions. It is important for the organization to recognize when it is important to use shared decision making and when a decision can be made unilaterally. Generally, two factors will influence that decision, time and impact. Occasionally, there will not be sufficient time and actions will need to be taken immediately. At other times, an issue will not have wide effect and only a few people will need to be consulted. In every case, however, it is important for decision makers to consider a variety of factors before a decision is made.

5. Consider the source of your information. The source may consciously or unconsciously present opinions as if they were facts. Whenever there are two sides to a story, do your best to obtain information from both sides of the argument. Remember that it is possible to have more than two sides and the alternatives should be considered.

6. Question everything, yet be open to all points-of-view. Sometimes the best solutions can come from individuals who have a new angle on the problem. Facts are essential to understand a problem and to evaluate proposed solutions. By digging to uncover and validate facts, we are better able to test the reliability and validity of our results and conclusions. (Goldman, 1990, p. G-2)

Problem Solving

One of the most important critical thinking skills is the ability to use systematic problem-solving techniques. Problem solving is a matter of changing some present set of conditions or circumstances to a desired set of conditions or circumstances. Accepting a most probable solution or reaching a reasonable decision can increase personal satisfaction and improve the quality of one's efforts and outcomes. This occurs because individuals decide what they want to have happen and then plan to make it happen. Efforts can be directed toward keeping the process moving in the right direction, and by anticipating possible pitfalls, major obstacles can be avoided.

People have tried to solve problems in many ways. A very popular but often ineffective technique is simple trial and error. Using this method, a person implements a series of possible solutions until a positive outcome results. A more effective problem-solving model has the following steps:

1. Determine your problem objectives
2. Gather facts
3. Identify obstacles to your objectives
4. Inventory your resources
5. Generate ideas for reaching your objectives
6. Make decisions
7. Take action

Figure 5.1 can be used as a worksheet to help use this model. In addition to these steps, Step 6—Make decisions—is a complex skill in its own right and requires further explanation.

When an eight-step decision-making process is added to the decision-making step of problem solving, a more complete picture of problem solving becomes visible. This decision-making model provides a procedure that people can use to help them make more effective decisions. The key issue is the effectiveness of the process. Every person makes hundreds of decisions every day. Some of these decisions are more effective than others, and some decisions are made by default. Default decisions occur as a result of not deciding and being left with whatever happens under the circumstances that exist. An example of a decision made by default is the person who hesitates in selecting a sale item, and someone else then buys the item. If that item is the last one available, the do-not-buy decision was made by default.

Problem solving is a matter of changing some present set of conditions to a desired set of conditions. The decisions you reach or the solutions you arrive at using the process described in this material can be many and varied.

Desired Outcome	Problem-Solving Steps
■ Increase satisfaction or improve quality	■ Determine your problem objectives
■ Decide what you want to happen	■ Gather facts
	■ Identify obstacles to your objectives
■ Plan to make it happen	■ Inventory your resources
■ Keep things going right	■ Generate ideas for reaching your objectives
■ Anticipate what is likely to happen	■ Make decisions
	■ Action steps

Figure 5.1. Problem solving.

The goal of a systematic decision-making model is to increase the probability that the outcomes of a decision will match those desired by the decision maker. Our suggested model includes the following steps:

1. *Define the problem:* State exactly what the problem is, or explain the situation and circumstances that may influence the decision.
2. *Consider all alternatives:* List all possible ways to solve the problem, or possible decisions that could be made. Information may need to be gathered so that all alternatives can be considered.
3. *Identify barriers to success for each alternative:* Identify the barriers that might interfere with successful resolution of the problem or with taking an effective course of action. Each barrier should be examined to determine if (a) the situation can be

altered, thus removing the barrier, or (b) there is nothing that can be done to change that circumstance.

4. *Consider the consequences of each alternative:* List all of the possible outcomes (both positive and negative) for each alternative or each course of action considered.

5. *Consider personal values:* Each decision made must be justified through a person's own value system. Values are based on our beliefs about how we should act and why we should behave that way.

6. *Choose one alternative:* Choose the alternative that is most appropriate based on your values, knowledge, present and future goals, and its effect on other people who are important to you.

7. *Implement the decision:* Do what is necessary to have the decision carried out the way you want it. It may be necessary to develop a step-by-step program with a timetable to make sure that things are done.

8. *Evaluate the outcome:* Examine the progress that you are making to see if what is happening is what you want to have happening. If you are not getting what you want, you will need to find out why and make the appropriate procedural modifications that will help you get on the right track. (Adapted from Goldman, 1990, p. G-5)

Organizationally, the main purpose of critical thinking and problem solving is to create the conditions for continuous improvement. As schools become more adept at organizational processes that encourage and enhance continuous improvement, they will take on a new dimension in their existence. That dimension will be built upon a model for organizational change. Where the schools of yesterday have desired stability, the schools of tomorrow will need to be dynamic. To succeed in this arena, schools will need to improve their ability to identify their problems, recognize their preferred solutions, and create effective action plans for successful implementation of strategies and programs. To achieve all of this, students need to be part of the problem-solving teams.

Applications

It is one thing to talk about creative and critical thinking. It is quite another to put both into action. In one rural Iowa school district, the

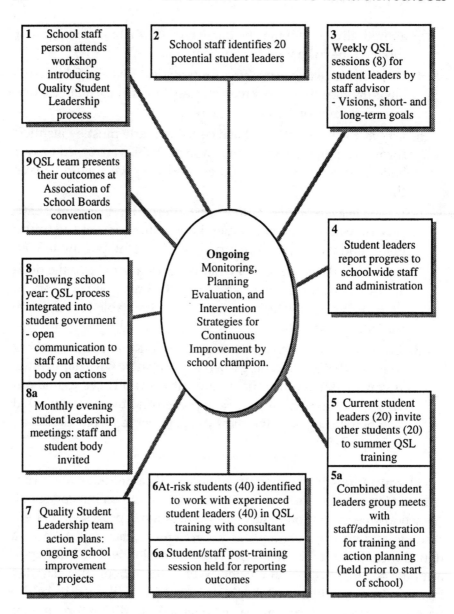

Figure 5.2. Master plan for student involvement.
Note: Phase 1 = 1-4; Phase 2 = 5-5a; Phase 3 = 6-7; Phase 4 = 8-9.

QSL process assisted in transforming the high school into a collaborative, problem-solving unit (see Figure 5.2). This district serves more than 1,600 students from five different attendance centers. The area consists of several small towns that are either agriculture/retirement based or bedroom communities for families that work in a nearby metropolitan area. The high school/middle school building serves

Grades 7 through 12 and approximately 750 students. The QSL project was implemented at the high school level by a teacher-counselor who was introduced to the process at a QSL workshop.

The staff of the school had identified 20 sophomores and juniors who were regarded as having leadership potential (#2, Figure 5.2), although they did not necessarily hold an elected office in student government. These 20 students attended weekly QSL training sessions (#3, Figure 5.2) that were led by the school's teacher-counselor. During that process, three general visions were developed, with numerous short- and long-term goals in each area. By the end of eight sessions, students reported their progress and visions to the staff and administration (#4, Figure 5.2), who had been working on similar tasks. Interestingly, the student and staff ideas were not significantly different. Terms used to describe the vision and goals were different depending upon each group's experiences and position, but they were philosophically the same.

These 20 students, who had decided to remain in the project, invited an additional 20 students to two training sessions held during the summer (#5, Figure 5.2). These students were identified by the previously trained cadre in order to achieve a more diverse representation for future problem-solving efforts. This larger group met for 2 full days of training and action planning with selected staff and administration (#5a, Figure 5.2). This workshop was held during the week prior to the start of school. Teachers and administrators were very impressed with the process and thoroughly enjoyed working with the students and talking on a one-to-one basis about issues that affect the educational process. The staff was surprised that students wanted the same things that the teachers did. This is a phenomenon that has been observed in many diverse settings. The students were surprised that the staff was willing to listen and be supportive of student ideas about making changes in the operation and programming in the school.

Later in the fall, after several short-term goals had been achieved successfully, another 40 students were added to the group. As a result of the problem-solving activities and the action plans that had been developed, it was decided that greater success could result from a broader student involvement. This next group of students was selected with the specific goal to increase representation by students who were identified as being at risk of not graduating from high school or were considered to be part of the disenfranchised. A facilitator of the QSL process spent a full day with these 40 new students and the 40 experienced students (#6, Figure 5.2). At the end of the day, a 75-minute session was held with all of the staff and some of those students.

In the months following the meeting with the students and the staff, the QSL process continued with a core of 65 students who made a commitment to the project and specific action plans (#7, Figure 5.2). For the remainder of that school year, progress was somewhat limited. A main reason for the limitations was that, although staff and administration were supportive, many did not connect with the student action planning. During the subsequent school year, however, the QSL project became more focused in the student government process (#8, Figure 5.2). The students followed the process and kept channels of communication open to the staff and any student who was interested in the action plans they created. Monthly meetings (#8a, Figure 5.2) were held so that students and staff could interact regarding the problem-solving activities and action-planning process. This also provided a vehicle for the continuous evaluation of progress and planning for improvements in the school and the processes used.

The value of this rural Iowa QSL project to the school was proportionate to the amount of commitment made by students and staff. When students and staff made commitments to the process, problems were identified, solutions were sought, and action plans were made. When only students were involved, the process stumbled. As students and staff worked together, the effectiveness of their actions vastly improved, and they experienced an enhanced ability to implement strategies and evaluate outcomes.

A significant indirect outcome of the project was the development of leadership and critical-thinking abilities on the part of participating students. As these students became effective leaders, they learned the value of being empathic listeners and supportive team members. The QSL process and training require that such skills be recognized, taught, learned, reinforced, and mastered. One of the rather insightful comments that came from this training was a reference to an administrative project that had not worked out as well as it might have. One of the QSL students commented, "You know why it didn't work very well, don't you? You did not have an action plan, only an idea."

As a result of this school's efforts, they were invited to participate in the Iowa Showcase at the Iowa Association of School Boards Conference (#9, Figure 5.2). More than 400 superintendents and school board members heard about the QSL project. Many of the participants indicated a strong interest in receiving more information on what this school had done and how they might be able to conduct a similar type of program in their own community. The display used was designed

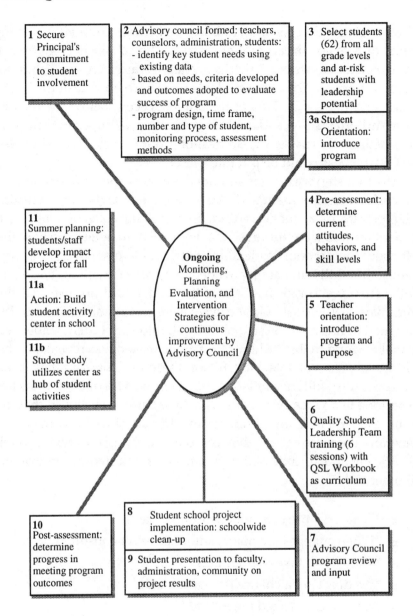

Figure 5.3. Master plan for student involvement.

by students from the school's QSL team. It featured the steps taken with pictures supporting the process and showing the implementation of the action plans that were made.

In a different setting, a different approach might be used. As an example, an inner-city magnet high school (Figure 5.3) that focuses on learning a broad-based curriculum through an emphasis on business and environmental studies used a much different approach. This school serves a diverse student body that comes from all major segments of a major urban school district. The school is composed of Hispanic, Asian, African American, Native American, and White students. More than 70% of the students were born outside of the United States, and more than 70% of the students score below the national norms in both reading and math. In this setting, as opposed to the rural Iowa setting, there was a great deal of groundwork to be laid before the QSL process could be put into place.

The first step was to gather data about how the students perceive their school environment and to determine where the school fits into their picture of a quality world. In this data collection phase, 62 student leaders were surveyed (#4, Figure 5.3) to determine how they felt about their school, leadership skills, problem-solving skills, communication skills, and ability to effectively plan for action. The results of the survey showed that 34% of the leaders did not feel that they were part of their school, and 55% were not involved in activities designed to improve the school. Why should the student leaders of a school respond in this fashion? Part of the reason was revealed in two additional pieces of data. First, 63% of these students said they lacked the leadership skills needed to participate, and 44% did not know how to be good team members. Although these students believed that they could help their fellow students in difficult situations, they were generally unaware of how they could make changes in their school.

The general attitude of the students was reflected in some of their comments:

- "I can't get projects done without a hassle."
- "When changes are made, students aren't consulted."
- "They don't take our opinion."
- "We don't get a chance [to participate]."
- "No one ever asked me to lead."
- "I never get to use them [decision-making skills]."

When students feel that they have been left out of the loop, there is little incentive to become part of the solution to the problems that exist. The events that followed this survey demonstrate how the QSL process can alter the course of a school and transform an environment of negativism into a quality environment.

Following the preassessment, the 62 student leaders went through a 6-week training program that used the QSL process (#6, Figure 5.3). The students represented all four high school grade levels, freshman to senior, and a diverse range of achievement categories: honor students, special education students, and classic underachievers. The group was also racially diverse, with representation from each of the ethnic subpopulations.

At the outset of this project, specific objectives were established. The staff and students used the results of the preassessment surveys to chart the path for the coming weeks (#7, Figure 5.3). The intended outcomes were the following:

1. To increase self-esteem through genuine accomplishment
2. To develop leadership skills
3. To learn how to communicate effectively
4. To increase cooperation and teamwork
5. To learn systematic critical thinking, problem solving, and creative thinking skills
6. To increase student involvement in the continuous improvement of the school

The first formal activity was a brainstorming session that focused on ways to make a difference in the high school's climate. As a result of that process, the students developed a vision for their Quality Leadership Tasks within their school. That vision was the "Motivation of Students and Staff Through (Quality) Student Leadership."

With a clear and focused mission, these students made a commitment to effecting change in their school culture. With that commitment came a decision that they must become goal oriented and that they should adhere, closely, to the QSL process. Central to the process is that participants plan and take action. To drive this planning and action phase, the students set several key goals:

1. [Increase the] motivation of students and teachers
2. Allow students to conduct assemblies for students (focusing on school improvement)
3. Conduct a series of student-teacher forums (to plan for a quality culture)
4. Promote schoolwide and communitywide support for sports teams to increase student and teacher involvement and possibly raise funds

Having identified goals was only a first step. A larger question loomed ahead for the students. What can be done to motivate the students and staff when so many efforts have failed before?

An important step in the problem-solving process is to recognize the obstacles that have the potential for undermining successful efforts. The students from this inner-city high school truly wanted to make a difference and had set reasonable goals for changing the school culture. To increase the chances for success, it was necessary that they take a careful look at those obstacles that could derail their efforts. Some of the obstacles they faced were the following:

1. No time was set aside for motivational activities.
2. No space was available for the QSL team meetings.
3. Students who wanted to help were only a small percentage of the total student population at the school.
4. Communication between staff and students did not exist outside of the classroom.
5. Students lacked the skills they needed to be successful.
6. Students lacked self-confidence.
7. Parents were uninvolved and did not understand what students were trying to do.
8. Gang involvement in and around school was intimidating.
9. Respect and support for one another was relatively low.

A key principle of the QSL process is to get students and teachers to realize that where there are deficits, there are also assets. If the focus is only on the deficits, the end product will likely be failure. Recognizing the assets—those resources that are available—moves the team toward neutralizing the negative impact of the obstacles.

To overcome the obstacles, these inner-city students decided to draw upon their strengths. They realized that they all had the ability to be creative and that they had the intelligence necessary to have an effect on their own worlds. They also recognized that there was a core of supportive teachers that could be relied upon to help them move forward. Furthermore, at this point in time, they were motivated to achieve their goals. To take the initial steps, they committed to using the free time they had built into their schedules, such as lunch and study hall, to do some of the groundwork necessary to start. In addition, the Local School Council had some funds that might be helpful, and certainly, local churches and community organizations would want to help improve the school. They could also enlist the help of special-interest, environmental groups. If they focused on projects that helped clean up the local environment, promoted environmental awareness, and had the potential for relatively immediate measurable gains, local advocates might lend a hand.

To best use the identified resources, the students decided to select a specific set of student leaders to direct the efforts. The immediate strategies to be implemented would be presented to the school at an all-school assembly to be attended by all students and teachers. The purpose of the assembly was to explain the service projects that would be conducted and to demonstrate how these projects would help the school and community. The assembly would also serve to build trust and promote mutual respect among all students and faculty. As a result of the assembly and the decision-making processes prior to and subsequent to the assembly, an improved attitude was observed. Greater participation and effort allowed the students and faculty to work together to achieve their goals.

As a first step toward the improvement of the high school, the students decided on a general school clean-up campaign (#8, Figure 5.3). This would demonstrate a team effort and provide a goal that could be accomplished within a reasonable amount of time. The students formed five teams to cover five different parts of the school with a leader appointed to coordinate activities in each section. Informational posters were put up throughout the building to let students and teachers know what was being planned. The principal sent out a memo to teachers and custodians to let them know about the clean-up activities. He then made sure that custodial closets were open so that students could get the cleaning supplies they needed. The principal also provided refreshments for everyone who worked on the project.

After the work was completed, a follow-up leadership session was held. During this session, the student leaders presented their impressions and issues to teachers, counselors, administrators, and community members (#9, Figure 5.3). As each of the five student work teams stood to speak, it was easy to see that it was a new experience to be the center of attention, speaking to a group of adults. Their confidence grew as they proceeded, and soon the students were communicating their thoughts and feelings with greater ease. They talked about their experience in going to various target areas of the school to clean up and how, in some areas, they were not allowed to work. The students felt that this happened because they were being treated like "little kids." They also pointed out, however, that they went on to other areas and worked as a team, in spite of their prior discouragement. They spoke of the need for more adult-student partnerships and activities to bring a renewed sense of family and unity. They clearly stated that they wanted to be involved in continuing to make a difference in their school. This session was attended by the wife of the city's deputy mayor. She commented, "I was quite surprised at how much I enjoyed this session. It was very real. You could see how far the students have come."

Eager to continue, as they stated in their presentation to the adults, these students took part in a summer planning session with key staff members (#11, Figure 5.3). This planning session was used to determine their next course of action. Following a brainstorming and action-planning session, it was clear that the priority goal was to build a student center at the school (#11a, Figure 5.3). After being challenged by the staff that this would take a considerable effort, the students still maintained their commitment to the idea. The students and a few staff members began building the center, which was located on the third floor of the high school, and it was completed several months later. It became an activity center for the entire student body and was operated by the QSL team (#11b, Figure 5.3).

Summary

Throughout this chapter, the focus has been on some of the basic skills students will need to be effective team members. Solving problems and planning for action require that young people have the ability to use creative and critical thinking. When these activities are conducted from a continuous improvement point of view, and when quality principles are applied, students experience greater success. When students are given the opportunity to use their natural abilities to be creative and ingenious, they produce. Even when faced by doubting adults, these students can and do demonstrate exceptional ability to analyze situations critically, make wise decisions, and create viable plans of action that generate positive change. If a school wishes to make the transition to quality, it is essential that the power of positive student thinking be unleashed. The transformations have been seen, and they are exciting. When students are empowered with the proper guidance and support of adult champions, the quality transformation is only a matter of time.

6

Evaluating Progress

We will no longer be measuring increases in output. That was important last month and we met the goal. This month we are going to measure on-time delivery, and I'd like your help reaching a new goal: to deliver exactly the kind of output needed by Dept. O within ten minutes of when they need it.

They set up new charts around the department and started the new measurements. Before long, with Joe doing the other things he now did—Zapp!—people began to behave in new ways. They began to think in terms of timeliness and specific need, rather than just volume.

—William Byham (1988, p. 111)

So often in education, daily business is conducted without much regard for what really is happening. After a certain amount of time, teachers generally get the notion that it is time to measure what has been done. Therefore, tests are given, scores are assigned, and grades are determined. Often, a student will say that the teacher gave him or her an "A" or a "C" or an "F." Teachers will respond, "I didn't give you anything—you earned your grade." Educators will go to great lengths to concoct systems by which students can remain constantly informed about their progress. In this way, they will not be surprised by the grade they earn. The truth is, however, that the adults still assign the grades.

From the small quotation above, from a marvelous book titled *Zapp!*, we begin to see the power of the worker taking responsibility for evaluating what is being done. At first, workers measured their output, and their output increased. Later, they measured timeliness and whether or not they were meeting a specific need of the department to which they were supplying their product. By measuring these new outcomes, a new level of quality was attained. It was not attained because management ordered it, but because management gave the workers the tools, skills, and opportunity to achieve the goals. Also interesting is that changing the goal did not eliminate the original goal; it just provided a new dimension for quality.

Students need a similar opportunity to learn how to measure their own progress. This is true whether we are talking about academic progress in the classroom or progress toward the successful completion of a task in a leadership activity. Measurements can be as simple as a thermometer to measure the money raised for student activities, or they can be more complex. One possible measure might be a statistical analysis of data collected regarding the relationship between student participation in leadership activities and student attendance rates. In either case, students need to be taught about the need to collect data, the way to collect data, and what can be done with the data once they are collected.

Measuring progress does two things for an action plan. First of all, it helps the team to stay on task. Much time can be wasted as teams become involved in nonproductive activities. Sometimes, team members will not even realize that what they are doing will not lead them toward their desired outcome. If measurements are being taken, however, team members can constantly ask themselves, What do these measurements mean? Are our efforts leading us toward our goal? If the actions we are taking are not taking us toward the desired outcome, what now?

A second important function of measurements is to let the team know how close it is coming to its goal. It is really helpful if the team is able to decide how much of a deviation from the exact goal is tolerable. If we are looking at a concept to be learned in a class, must the students get the concept 100% correct 100% of the time, or 85% correct 100% of the time, or 100% correct 85% of time, etc.? If we are making a product, can the product be off by .001 cm, or by .5 degrees, or can it be around 100 inches long? It is important to know not only what the target is but also how big it is. Once these standards have been set, student teams can continuously assess their progress toward the goal.

In education, there are often goals that seem to be immeasurable. For example, how do you measure an attitude, a belief, or an appreciation? For several years, education gurus have advised school personnel to avoid these types of goals because they are unmeasurable. We believe, however, that these goals are very worthy of measurement. To make these measurements, we simply need to be a little creative.

The first step in measuring these so-called intangible goals is to determine why we are even interested in this as a goal. Why do we care whether a group of students has a "good" or "bad" attitude? Perhaps it is because our experience has been that students with a positive attitude about school tend to be on time and are generally prepared for class. They also attend more regularly and have fewer conflicts with their teachers. By making this simple analysis of why we want to know about student attitudes, we have identified the behaviors in which we are most interested. Now, when these behaviors are measured, it might be possible to assume that the attitude has improved. In reality, however, it does not make much difference. If it is determined that the environment and culture of the school have improved, changed attitudes are no longer the issue. We can now be satisfied that conditions are better.

How Data Can Be Used

Let's look at an example of a situation that involved a combined teacher-student task team at Sturgis High School. This team had been working to improve student work habits. The team was composed of approximately 10 teachers and 10 students who had dedicated themselves to improving work habits in the school. Specifically, they wanted to increase the percentage of students completing assignments and turning them in on time. Initially, a strategy was identified.

Freshmen would be targeted, and all freshmen would be required to carry a three-ring binder notebook in which they would keep their assignments from each class. Teachers measured whether or not students brought their notebooks to class. Once every other week, at various times of the day, teachers were asked to measure whether students had their assignments completed and whether they were turning them in on time. The data collected indicated that students were carrying their required notebooks, but the completion rate and on-time rate for assignments was unaffected. It was eventually decided that this strategy was ineffective, and a new strategy was developed.

The second strategy was to require that freshmen keep an assignment book. The books were purchased for the students and distributed on the first day of school. Once again, measurements were taken, and it was discovered that students would carry the assignment book, but that the completion and promptness rate for the assignments were not affected. Again, the team decided that the strategy was not working.

At this point, the team asked why these students were not doing their work. The students on the committee had a good answer to the question. Apparently, most students found the schoolwork to be meaningless and boring. The students who completed the work anyway had specific goals for their life and saw an education as being very important for achieving those life goals. Those who did not do their work either tended not to have any life goals, or they did not see a connection between success in school and achieving their life goals.

Armed with this new information, the team went about its task in an entirely new way. The goal was the same, but the way to achieve the goal had changed. The goal was no longer an attempt to coerce the students into completing the work and getting it in on time, but rather finding out how the school could make the work more satisfying for the student. It was decided that a strong partnership between the school and the local business community would be very helpful. If students could see how they could apply what they were learning in real-world situations, they would be more apt to learn the material. In addition, through partnerships, students would have a chance to explore careers that might help them focus on what they wanted to do in the future.

Finally, the data began to show improvement. More students were completing their homework and getting it turned in on time. Simultaneously, the GPA from the freshman class increased, and attendance improved. Measuring the outcomes of the strategies applied allowed the team to modify what was being done and continues to help the team set new directions for the future.

It is also important to understand that not all measurements will seem to be quantifiable measurements. There will be times when a measurement will be nothing more than a recognition of how students feel about a situation or how teachers feel about the overall atmosphere of the school. Even so, we can quantifiably collect this data. How many students describe an experience in a certain way, or how many teachers believe that school environment is at this or that level? As we implement certain plans, we can see how these data change and then evaluate effectiveness based on these assessments.

Establishing Baselines

To know whether or not a school has made progress on a specific goal, that school must know where it began. Any single goal will identify one or more characteristics of a quality culture that will need to be improved over the time of focus. By identifying those characteristics, a school creates the basis for a preassessment that can be done to determine the beginning point. At Sturgis High School, the key quality characteristics were identified as informational reading, problem solving, tolerance for diversity, work habits, and a sense of belonging. For each of these, specific questions were created to be used in a preassessment survey. The survey was distributed to faculty, students, parents, and community members. This survey provided the data needed to begin developing strategies for effecting change. It also became a basis for comparison at the completion of a 7-year school improvement process.

Throughout the process of continuous quality improvement, it is necessary that measurements be made. With each measurement, several things happen. First of all, the quality improvement team begins to see a picture of how the strategy is affecting the key quality characteristic. Part of the quality improvement philosophy is dependent upon the ability to correct a course when it is appropriate. If a strategy is ineffective, it needs to be modified or abandoned. To keep on doing something because it's in the plans, when it is not yielding the results you are looking for, is wasteful and frustrating. Quality organizations look for evidence of the effectiveness of their efforts and are willing to adjust when necessary. This is precisely why students need to learn how to use the Plan-Do-Study-Act cycle. It is also why students need to learn how to collect data, analyze data, and represent that data using tables and graphs.

A second by-product of the continuous measurement process is that what gets measured gets done. When a quality improvement team takes on the responsibility for measuring progress at regular intervals, that team maintains its focus on both the strategy and the goal. Without this focus, it is possible to put the strategy and the goal on a shelf and ignore it over time. To create a quality culture, members of the team must be committed to the achievement of the goal. Measurement, and the focus it brings, helps team members see that something is, indeed, being done. Even if a strategy is not successful, at least the team knows that an effort is being made and that that effort is based on careful study and planning regarding this key characteristic. Nothing deflates a team faster than inaction. For most students and educators, the fact that dreams are being acted on is enough to demonstrate that what the team values is what the school values. This helps to maintain a level of motivation that ensures that the work will continue.

Empowering Student Leaders to Do Research and to Act on What They Find!

During the years that the QSL programs have been conducted, numerous teams in a variety of schools have applied the principles of quality leadership. These teams have seen progress made toward establishing a quality culture. Some of these schools have been discussed in previous chapters. Sturgis High School, one of the pioneers in QSL, has been used frequently as a model of how students can transform their school culture. Being able to collect, analyze, and report data in a way that vividly describes the transformation has been essential in each of these schools.

At Sturgis High School, students collected data regarding opinions and feelings about the overall sense of acceptance and belonging experienced by their fellow students. This survey was comprehensive and was distributed to every student during a homeroom session. More than 600 surveys were returned and analyzed by the staff/ student teams. This exercise taught the students several lessons, the least of which was not that random sampling techniques have a distinct advantage over sampling the entire population. Conceptually, the students learned that it was not all the teachers' and administrators' fault when students did not feel accepted and welcome at the high school; they found that the way students treated each other was equally significant in whether or not a student felt welcome. (See Appendix C for a copy of this survey.)

Considering their findings, the staff/student teams made several recommendations for changes in the structure of the school. Among these were the following:

1. Revise the student disciplinary process to make it more instructional rather than punitive.

2. Provide opportunities for students to be recognized for the efforts they make as well as for achievement.

3. Create a system for conflict resolution that can help to avoid violence.

4. Create an ongoing student leadership development program so that the process does not stop when current student leaders graduate.

5. Create a system where students can help students with both social and academic problems.

Based on these recommendations, several strategies were developed. A new approach to student behavior management was adopted that was based on the application of Dr. William Glasser's Choice Theory, Reality Therapy, and Quality Schools approach. A recognition program was established that recognized students for doing what they needed to do to succeed. The emphasis on achievement was removed because every person needs the opportunity to try something new and challenging without the fear of failure. The peer listener team was transformed into a peer assistance team. Team members served as mediators during conflict and as listeners when students just needed to unburden their hearts. A Quality Student Leadership Club was created that allows any student to work toward the continuous improvement of the high school. This team meets on a regular basis and is currently planning to schedule a series of leadership workshops and seminars for students. Finally, to address the need for academic assistance, the students created the peer tutoring team. These students actually go into the classroom and work hand in hand with teachers to help students understand and achieve. These students give up a block of their time schedule to assist the teacher in achieving academic goals.

In the 7 years since this program began, Sturgis High School has seen dramatic improvements in student behavior, attendance rates, and standardized test scores. Best of all, the overall atmosphere of the school has been extremely positive. It is hard to tie each of these improvements directly to the original QSL process, but there is a definitive line that separates the pre-QSL years from the post-QSL years. In addition, the primary changes made were changes that stemmed from the teams created after those first QSL workshops conducted in the spring of 1991. Although each team developed its own strategies, those strategies were developed in the way they were only because of the input from students on the staff/student teams.

Sturgis, fortunately, is not the only success story. There are several schools in the northwestern region of Iowa that were trained in the QSL process. These students learned how to collect and interpret data in a way that would lead to informed and constructive decision making. There were staff/student teams trained in Kentucky who took their skills back to their schools and created plans for making the Quality Transformation. These students also learned how to collect and use data to make better decisions about the future of their schools. Most significant, however, has been the involvement of several schools in Chicago. Students in those schools have learned and have been able to accomplish quality improvement goals even though the cards have been stacked against them.

In the second largest high school in Chicago (Chicago Vocational High School, or CVS), students felt that the community had a bad impression of them. They wanted to change that image by showing that they could be an asset to the community. To support this vision, the principal invited 100 students to discuss the needs of the school. The principal told them, "You have a responsibility to make this school a little better because you are here. You have the power to transform this school."

The students identified the key characteristics they wanted to change and formed seven student teams to specifically address the issues, develop action plans, and implement them. Teams of students, with the guidance of staff advisors and the coaching of consultants trained in the QSL process, began implementing action plans in the school and community. These teams also conducted a series of assemblies designed to inform all students about their vision and the actions they would take.

Student teams created and conducted staff and student surveys to assess present conditions and attitudes in the school and community. As a consequence of the survey results, they held meetings to elicit support from parents, shared their plans with elementary students and teachers, developed a peer helper system, organized fundraisers, and directed a school beautification project. The team also removed graffiti, painted bathrooms, and posted student volunteers at strategic points in the halls to monitor security. They called themselves US, for United Students. They came to realize that they had to take responsibility for their school culture if positive change was to occur.

As the student leadership concept expanded, they focused on outreach into the local community. This was done to make employment opportunity contacts and to heighten business awareness of the resources available at the school and the needs that were yet to be met.

Parents were stunned by the turnaround. The PTA president stated, "Students are trying to upgrade the school. It's important for parents to roll up their sleeves and help out." Students now seem more excited about school, and parent involvement, once nearly nonexistent, is starting to show signs of significant improvement, with more parents volunteering to serve on school improvement committees.

Feeling that things were getting better does not mean that they are, indeed, better. The students needed a way to show local school officials and community leaders that they were making a difference. A large time investment was being made, and the way things were being done was definitely a change. Change is not comfortable. Thus, if the process was to continue, the students needed to be able to demonstrate, through the use of collected data, that the changes made were resulting in positive and measurable outcomes. One method of evaluating progress was the use of graphs. Students were trained in the basic procedures for transforming data into meaningful graphs. The school's art and drafting departments helped the students create graphs that would not only tell the story but would also catch the attention of an audience. This team of trained data interpreters and graph developers chose the types and layouts for graphs to be developed. Members were assigned as liaisons to the other task teams in order to collect the necessary data. They also made sure that the data were brought to the data and graph team with enough time to prepare their presentation. Because of this focus on the measurement and reporting of progress, each task team was moved forward toward its stated mission.

As everyone is fully aware, no project comes off without a hitch. To address the obstacles to progress of the specialized task teams, a Quality Assurance Plan was developed. This plan identified student leaders who were trained as liaisons to carry information to and from the Quality Student Management Team (QSMT). In this way, the communication between the QSMT and the individual task teams was continuous and uninterrupted. These quality assurance liaisons ensured a consistency of quality with respect to goal progress and attainment. The mechanism by which this process was carried out is shown in Figures 6.1 and 6.2. This strategy was designed to empower the school's stakeholders to self-manage the student involvement process and to progressively become independent of the external consultant in the school improvement effort.

Through the use of the liaisons, specific issues and gaps in the process were discovered. This information was then used to provide specific training in the identified areas of concern. It was found that

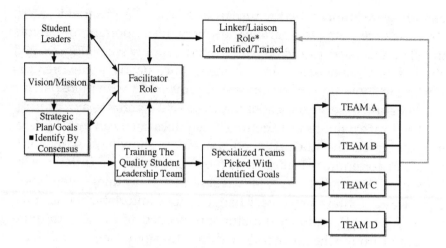

Figure 6.1. Quality assurance process.
Note: * See Liaison Report, Figure 6.2.

		Measurable Progress	Obstacles Encountered	Intervention Delivered	Next Steps	Comments
G O A L #1	Date					
G O A L #2	Date					
G O A L #3	Date					

Team Name: - - - - - - - - - - - - - - - - - Meeting Date: - - - - - - - Contact Person/Team Leader: -

Reported to Graphing representative for logging on ___/___/___

Figure 6.2. Liaison report out form.

students needed additional training in developing a mission, setting goals, creating action plans, setting and adhering to timelines, and leading teams. Once this additional training was completed, an ongoing flow of supporting data was established, and meaningful graphs of progress could be developed. These graphs were brought back to each team for any final changes and updates that were needed and were then posted for all stakeholders to see (see Figures 6.3, 6.4, and 6.5). This strategy gave everyone a clear idea as to how the implemented plans were affecting the school and to what extent progress

---

You Can't Manage What You Can't Measure

It is strongly recommended that all quality improvement projects be not only measured but illustrated graphically. Graphs have the power to quickly communicate progress. An up-to-date graph is like a speedometer in a car, in fact it feeds back to the driver exactly how he or she is performing at any given time and thereby serves as a guide to decision making and action. Graphs and illustrations also have the power to motivate people to perform better by involving them in the process.

Here is a simplified procedure for measuring and graphing your quality improvement progress:

1. Decide what you wish to measure, such as attendance, parent involvement, student achievement, etc.

2. Decide what you wish to measure it against, such as time, money or efforts.

3. Determine how you will gather data on the current situation, such as observation, counting, using special forms, etc.

4. Set "SMART" objectives or outcomes - Specific, Measurable, Attainable, Reasonable and Trackable, such as "Increase attendance by 5%".

5. Arrange your data using appropriate statistical methods and various graphing formats, such as bar graphs, line graphs or flow charts (see Resource A).

6. Prominently display your graphs.

7. Update your graphs at regular intervals.

Figure 6.3.

was being made toward the improvement of the school's Quality Culture. This provided an excellent opportunity for members of one team to support the progress made by other teams and to have their own progress validated through the support of others. It also provided an opportunity for those who were not part of the process to become involved.

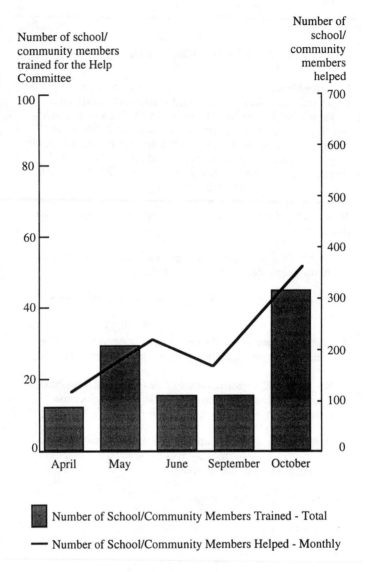

Figure 6.4. Student leadership team graph.

The 6-month, start-up, student involvement process was successful in that it created a new awareness on the part of both students and
adults of what our young people could accomplish. A cadre of student
leaders received training and follow-up support in implementing
projects in the school and community. As the principal exclaimed,

The magic is happening here at CVS! Everyone in the school is
excited about the possibilities of what can occur with students,
staff, parents, and community involvement. The whole atmos-

Function/Player	1	2	3	4	5	6	7	8
School/Community Beautification								
Task 1								
Task 2								
Task 3								
Peer Counseling								
Task 1								
Task 2								
Task 3								
Community Outreach								
Task 1								
Task 2								
Task 3								

Allows the user to "see" each team's responsibilities, puts in perspective the whole process, and prevents overlapping

Figure 6.5. Student leadership team graph.

phere of the school has changed because people are working together toward a common vision, creating real results that are impacting the quality of education at CVS.

An involved student said, "I am proud to attend CVS. I want other people to feel proud of the school, too." From the success, feedback, and evaluations during this phase of the project, we feel that more of the community can be proud of the school and its students.

The next step was a comprehensive approach toward quality education where the school's nonstudent stakeholders (parents, teachers, community members, and administration) became involved. The student leadership team involvement was the catalyst for creating an entire community improvement initiative. During the completion of the project, the U.S. Department of Education nominated 24 Illinois schools as National Blue Ribbon Schools. Three Chicago schools were chosen for this honor, with Chicago Vocational High School being one of them. All schools were eligible to submit a nomination based on criteria that included student achievement, administrative leadership, vision and goals, learning environment, curriculum, and student dropout rate. The selection of CVS was certainly a reflection and solid acknowledgment of the dedicated work and progress of the entire school community.

Most recently, in 1997, the U.S. Department of Education se-lected CVS as one of five High Schools of the Future in the United States. These five schools are being used to create the model urban high school for the 21st century. Using the total school community team approach, including students, that was emphasized during the initial quality improvement (QSL) process, CVS has continued to integrate additional innovations. Their hard work and perseverance has transformed this school into a showcase and resulted in this recognition.

7

Student Leadership in Future Learning Communities

Youth need to see themselves as valued members of a group that offers mutual support and trusting relationships. They need to become socially competent individuals who have the skills to cope successfully with everyday life. They need to believe that they have a promising future.

—Carnegie Council on Adolescent Development (1989)

Schools need to be thought of as open systems. If systems are considered in the organic sense, schools would be observed as an assemblage of similar structures and elements that combine for the same general function. As an open system, those components are as easily affected from without as they are from within. In turn, those parts not only have internal relevance but also have meaning beyond the system.

Once schools are regarded as systems, society will begin to understand the need for constant maintenance and care for the system. Systems generally take in raw materials, modify them through some process, and create a product. Because a school "system" is composed of many interdependent subsystems, each with its own raw materials, processes, and products, the very nature of the school "system" is extremely complex. The complexity of the system, however, does not detract from the need to continuously improve the processes by which products are made.

To better understand this concept, it might be beneficial to take a look at the typical raw materials, processes, and products of an educational system. Overall, the raw materials are children, and the products are adults who can positively contribute to their community, state, country, and the world. The process includes all of the content, methods, and procedures of schooling. American society needs to stop complaining about the inputs and outputs of the system and start focusing on ways of making the system more efficient and effective. When the American educational system is compared to the systems in Europe and Asia, there is a continuous reminder of how well those systems work. It appears that their systems are more effective than ours. It is often heard that Japan, Korea, and Germany send their students to school more days per year, and more hours per day, than do American schools; plus, they spend more money per student. It appears that the American system may be more efficient than theirs.

This appears to have been a typical American methodology: too much focus on the efficiency bottom line and not enough on the effectiveness bottom line. Successful schools of tomorrow will pay close attention to both effectiveness and efficiency. In a Quality Student Leadership (QSL) school, the processes of the system become the main focus. The processes begin to wrap around to include all aspects of the community in the redevelopment of what schools should be. To reshape schools means that society must be reshaped. It is a simple matter of values. The society that places very high value on education and has high expectations for educational progress will achieve what it wants. At this point in time, American society has not made such a commitment to education.

In addition to an inadequate commitment to education in American society, American students, in general, begin at a deficit when compared to students in other developed nations. Herbert Walberg refers to this symptom as the "Matthew Effect" (Walberg, 1988). Although the reference focused on disparities between students in American schools, it aptly applies to the disparity between American and Japanese schools. The Matthew Effect essentially recognizes that students who start off school with an academic advantage make larger gains than do students who do not have the same advantages. Thus, the rich get richer and the poor get poorer. We contend that the academically rich are rich because of the underlying values those cultures bring to the academic arena. If American schools are going to compete in global academics, they will need to be spawned from a new society that places a higher value on its educational system. In doing so, the blaming stops and the problem solving begins.

The school system of tomorrow is an inclusive, rather than an exclusive, system. It involves *students*, parents, community members, teachers, administrators, and support staff in trying to solve the complex problems that presently exist. The schools of tomorrow are a birth-to-death endeavor. They are life giving and responsive to the needs of all members of society. Graduations as they exist today will be unnecessary in tomorrow's schools. All people will realize that learning is a lifelong process that never ends, and thus, we merely have levels of understanding that are reached. The Quality Leadership School will recognize that the system is the way we get things done, and if things do not get done the way we would like them to be done, the system needs to be improved.

To make the transformation from input focus to system focus, schools are beginning to pay attention to successful businesses. In some ways, this is good, but in other ways, this could be very bad. There are those that advocate operating schools like successful businesses. To many, this seems like an excellent idea, and it may be in some cases, but there are some dramatic differences between schools and most businesses. In addition, some businesses are successful in spite of the way they treat employees and customers.

The most significant difference between schools and business is the fact that a business will exist only for as long as it can produce a valuable product or service for its customers. Schools, on the other hand, provide a service that, at best, can offer only a deferred benefit to its ultimate customers, the students. In business, the customer sees immediate usefulness for the product or service it has purchased. In schools, the usefulness of what is taught and learned may not be evident for several years. For schools to be successful, it is essential that the school experience fulfill valuable student needs. Because the power and freedom that result from the knowledge, abilities, and skills that children acquire may not be realized for some time, schools must meet other needs through the academic endeavors of their students. This means that they must find ways to create experiences that offer relevance to what students must learn. Most notably, fulfilling the needs of fun and belonging can help make school a more satisfying place. These needs can be met by providing direct application for learning activities through service learning projects and integrated curricular offerings. These experiences will have a lasting impact and will help students develop the skills that have been identified as critical for future employment. Through the efforts of a QSL educational system, students will learn to enjoy learning, and they will gain a sense of belonging within this great American society. Students will find real value in what they can contribute to society and what, in turn, they can reap from their efforts.

Perhaps one of the greatest dangers in trying to emulate the successful business in schools is the fact that systems of education are rarely as neat and tidy in their operational scheme as are highly successful businesses. The greatest similarity is that both effective schools and successful businesses have inputs, processes, and outputs. Businesses, however, provide specifications to their suppliers concerning the qualities they need in the inputs. Schools must work with whatever they get. Businesses will process their inputs to create the best output possible. If a specific output does not meet standards, the responsible process can be modified in a continuous attempt to improve the quality of the output. An important goal is to eliminate as many variables as possible. Schools are also evaluating outputs for quality and, in fact, are evaluating progress continuously. There is a major problem, however, when schools try to determine where the process is deficient. When we try to help students learn, we are dealing with a multidimensional process that is affected by numerous variables, some of which have yet to be identified. Therefore, it becomes extremely difficult for schools to emulate successful businesses.

The situation is not hopeless. What schools can do is learn from successful businesses and use that knowledge to create better educational processes. It would be dangerous to copy business practices in the educational setting, but it makes sense to borrow and use the parts that fit. A major pitfall to avoid is the paradigm paralysis that would keep schools from examining how some best practices might apply in a particular educational setting. Successful businesses have approached the problem of falling productivity and inadequate quality by having workers evaluate their processes and products continually. Schools can teach students to do the same. If there is a better way to learn how to do something, students can help find that medium. Problem solving should become a collaborative activity that involves everyone in the school community. Decision making needs to be shared among all stakeholders in the system. Finally, the focus must become the process rather than the people, because as long as the educational community focuses on people, there is a tendency to fix the blame rather than the problem.

CHAMPS: Communities Honoring Achieving, Motivated, Positive Students

In any situation, the goal of school transformation is to create a culture that promotes student learning and success. In many schools, the existing culture is one that has not learned how to celebrate success and has learned too well how to identify and chastise failure. If success begets success, our first charge is to create a culture that focuses on success and diminishes the negative connotation of failure. This is where CHAMPS becomes a critical component of the school transformation process. Figure 7.1 is the Quality Improvement Associates (QIA) mission statement. In this figure, the CHAMPS life skills are shown to be applicable across the total school community areas of schools, community, corporations, colleges, and government. It is a whole school community process in which adults and students work in an action-oriented partnership that will shape student character, performance, and social responsibility.

Rather than looking for the things that students do wrong, CHAMPS looks for opportunities to recognize students for their honest efforts to make their world a better place. Sometimes, the efforts made will have minimal returns, but the critical issue is that the students took the risk to make a difference. Through the CHAMPS process, students learn a practical and real application of the old adage "nothing ventured, nothing gained," and at the same time, they learn that failure is not fatal.

CHAMPS is intended to turn each school into a learning community and serves as an umbrella for student empowerment models. Throughout this book, a Master Plan has been presented that shows how the process can work in different school settings. Perhaps the single most important reason to use either QSL or Quality Student Learning as a student empowerment model is that each is adaptable to any setting. Because no two communities or schools are identical, it is important that the process is adaptable to the conditions that exist. There are, however, some standard activities that apply to all environments. These activities are used to assist in directing efforts while more specific plans are made. CHAMPS is one of the mechanisms used to enlist the support of an entire community for students who have been trained in one of these two processes.

There are some fundamental elements that should be in place when considering the creation of a learning community. Failure to provide for these needs in a setting could result in wasted time, energy, and effort. These elements are the following:

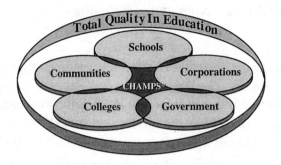

Quality Improvement Associates Mission

Champion For Students

*QIA champions and educates young people and
adults through a dynamic process that builds
strong leaders and lifelong learners*

*It engages them in authentic experiences to face
the critical challenges in their lives, schools, and
community*

*Students demonstrate positive actions, through
committed partnerships, that shape mature
character, academic performance, and social
responsibility*

*Communities Honor Achieving, Motivated, Positive Students

Figure 7.1. Mission statement.

1. A project coordinator and consultant(s) should be available to each school community. They should assist and support participants as they work to create a learning community.

2. Ongoing assessment of the school's learning community is needed to determine training and support needs.

3. It is necessary to have a clear focus on curriculum and instruction as they relate to broader quality school improvement goals.

4. The program used must be flexible enough to address the unique needs of diverse school communities.

5. The learning community must have clearly defined and expected outcomes, as well as the processes in place for creating strategies to achieve those outcomes.

6. All stakeholders, including students, must be involved in the planning. This is best accomplished when a specific plan has been created for including the stakeholders.

When these elements are present and the CHAMPS process is in place, a marvelous transformation in the school and the learning community takes place. The following projects were conducted using the QSL program (in a rural middle school) and the Quality Student Learning program (in two inner-city elementary schools), along with the CHAMPS process. We truly believe that the combination of QSL and CHAMPS creates an environment that allows high-risk populations to succeed when other approaches have failed.

Carnegie Foundation Middle School Project

In 1989, under the auspices of the Carnegie Council on Adolescent Development, the Task Force on Education of Young Adolescents produced *Turning Points: Preparing American Youth for the 21st Century*. The report describes the middle grade schools as being "potentially, society's most powerful force to recapture millions of youth adrift, and [they] help every young person thrive" (p. 8). It urges restructuring of the middle grades as an antidote to the traditional junior high school. The report states that "there is a volatile mismatch between the organization and curriculum of middle school grades, and the intellectual and emotional needs of young adolescents" (p. 8).

A fundamental transformation of the education of our young people is required. The middle grade school proposed in the Carnegie Report is profoundly different from many schools today. The Carnegie Middle School focuses on the needs of young adolescents. It creates a community of adults and young people embedded in the networks of support that enhance the commitments of students to learning.

To follow up on its 1989 report, the Carnegie Council created the Middle Grade School State Policy Initiative in 1990. This initiative provided planning and implementation grants to 27 states to implement their eight recommendations:

1. Create small communities for learning.
2. Teach a core of common knowledge.
3. Ensure success for students.
4. Empower teachers and administrators.

5. Specifically prepare teachers for teaching middle-grade students.

6. Improve academic performance through better health and fitness.

7. Reengage families in the education of young adolescents.

8. Connect schools with communities.

At the time of this initiative, a small southern Illinois town of 20,000 people began looking for a new approach for educating their middle-grade students. Dissatisfied with the progress being made by these young adolescent students in their traditional junior high school setting, the principal was looking for an innovative means for transforming the school. The district approached the Illinois State Board of Education and was invited to participate in the Carnegie Initiative (Figure 7.2).

The principal spoke of his commitment to changing the educational paradigm from that of passivity to one of active student participation in the learning process. It was believed that students should become actively involved in the workings and doings of the classroom, school, and community. The groundwork for student empowerment was already established by a teacher who became the champion for the cause. The true challenge was changing school norms from teacher-directed to student-centered, active learning. The principal and the champion both welcomed the QSL approach. It was an established process for empowering young people and transforming the school culture, yet it was flexible and adaptable to the school's unique needs and environment.

As a kick-off activity, a half-day student leadership training workshop was scheduled. This workshop was conducted for identified potential student leaders who would present the outcomes of their planning to the school's faculty. It was agreed that this would be a dynamic introduction to the student empowerment process. At the core of the QSL process is teaching young people how to dream and then how to translate that dream into a vision. During this leadership workshop, the students developed this vision:

We, the students . . . have a vision to be seen for what we are, separate individuals. We should be trusted and respected as we trust and respect others. We will communicate with one another, take risks, participate in school activities, support student empow-

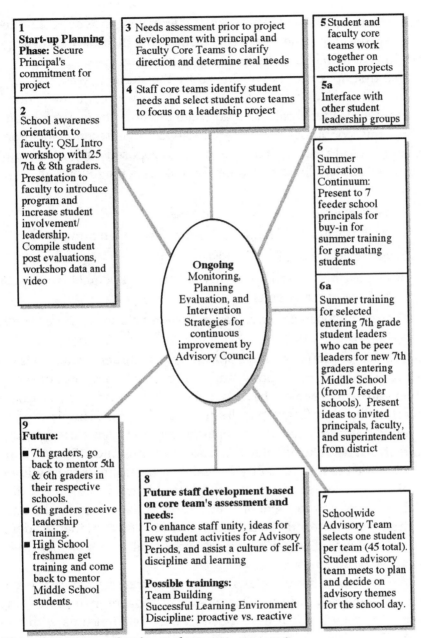

1
Start-up Planning Phase: Secure Principal's commitment for project

2
School awareness orientation to faculty: QSL Intro workshop with 25 7th & 8th graders. Presentation to faculty to introduce program and increase student involvement/ leadership. Compile student post evaluations, workshop data and video

3 Needs assessment prior to project development with principal and Faculty Core Teams to clarify direction and determine real needs

4 Staff core teams identify student needs and select student core teams to focus on a leadership project

5 Student and faculty core teams work together on action projects

5a
Interface with other student leadership groups

Ongoing Monitoring, Planning Evaluation, and Intervention Strategies for continuous improvement by Advisory Council

6
Summer Education Continuum: Present to 7 feeder school principals for buy-in for summer training for graduating students

6a
Summer training for selected entering 7th grade student leaders who can be peer leaders for new 7th graders entering Middle School (from 7 feeder schools). Present ideas to invited principals, faculty, and superintendent from district

9
Future:
■ 7th graders, go back to mentor 5th & 6th graders in their respective schools.
■ 6th graders receive leadership training.
■ High School freshmen get training and come back to mentor Middle School students.

8
Future staff development based on core team's assessment and needs:
To enhance staff unity, ideas for new student activities for Advisory Periods, and assist a culture of self-discipline and learning

Possible trainings:
Team Building
Successful Learning Environment
Discipline: proactive vs. reactive

7
Schoolwide Advisory Team selects one student per team (45 total). Student advisory team meets to plan and decide on advisory themes for the school day.

Figure 7.2. Master plan for student empowerment.
Note: Phase 1 = 1-5a; Phase 2 = 6-7; future phases = 8 and 9.

erment, and work together to achieve a common goal. We agree to encourage and motivate one another.

As the students reviewed their vision, they recognized that they were presented with specific challenges. Rather than view these challenges as problems, the students approached the challenges as opportunities to demonstrate that they were capable of using their new knowledge and skills to help build a better learning community.

The first opportunity recognized by the students was that there seemed to be a "lack of mutual respect and two-way communication." The student leaders brainstormed some possible strategies for combating this condition and then developed five recommendations through critical analysis of the many ideas proposed during the brainstorming activity. These recommendations were the following:

1. Give teachers reasons to respect us.
2. Both teachers and students need to have open minds.
3. Share how we feel with our teachers.
4. Get teachers to talk to us privately instead of embarrassing us in front of our friends.
5. Promote open communication between students and teachers.

Vital to the creation of an environment where students want to learn is the existence of open, honest, and caring communication. Too many schools are so focused on the academic and behavior aspects of school operation that they forget that all student behavior is a simple attempt to fulfill needs. When the personal needs of students are ignored, students see no value in what the school is doing, and without value, there is little interest in quality. If schools want students to be willing to take the risks necessary to contribute to the development of a quality school culture, schools must address the whole student. As these students have indicated, there is more to a student than academics and athletics. The psychological, emotional, and spiritual needs must also be addressed.

For a school to take the steps necessary for transformation to occur requires some risk. Adults risk exposure of some of their underlying feelings as they become more open in their relationships with students. They also risk losing control over the school because students will now be empowered to voice their opinions and participate in decision making. These risks, however, are well worth taking because they promote a more positive emotional connection between the students and the school. This results in a greater sense of belonging and of personal power for the students—two essential human needs. The students felt more at ease with themselves and more motivated to achieve and do quality work. They also recognized that it was all right to make mistakes—responsible people learn from their mistakes and make plans for avoiding them in the future. This continuous improvement ethic is a cornerstone of the QSL process.

Once the students had been trained and the staff was accepting of this new relationship, the real work began. The students brainstormed old and new paradigms concerning how students view adults and how students believe adults see them. Some of the new paradigms are listed below.

New Ways for Students to See Adults

1. Pay attention to what adults say.
2. Follow directions.
3. Try to understand adults.
4. Discuss problems with adults.
5. Take responsibility.

New Ways for Adults to See Students

1. Young people can think for themselves.
2. Students can make decisions and face problems.
3. Ask young people for their ideas.
4. Young people can be trusted.
5. Be fair to all students.

After presenting these ideas of new paradigms for their school, the students were asked to suggest new ways for adults and students to work together. The students shared, and the staff listened. One of the critical issues was fairness, which is part of feeling respected and valued as potential contributors to the school. This sense of fairness incorporates integrity. Students know when integrity is being demonstrated in a classroom, either by the teacher or by other students. Integrity produces a sense of "we're all in this together." In other words, integrity creates a true community.

The student presentation to the faculty demonstrated the expected outcomes for the QSL workshop and the CHAMPS process. That presentation shared the students' perceptions of old and new paradigms, their vision for student empowerment in the school, key challenges that students will face, and recommendations as to how to deal with these challenges. They also suggested activities that could be used during advisory periods to help all students develop leadership skills. Not surprising, many of these ideas stemmed from their experiences in the QSL workshop. The presentation time culminated in a public declaration of commitment to student empowerment by the faculty. Partnerships between students and staff were created, and the entire group then became involved in an in-depth question-and-answer session.

As a result of the student presentation, one of the faculty teams decided to create a student action team. This team would encourage students who were facing problems to accept personal responsibility for their lives and not to use their problems as an excuse to display inappropriate behaviors. Even though the faculty created the team without a preconceived plan for its operation, the main goal was to recognize positive behaviors and enlist student input and energy to help make classrooms and the school a better place. This team created a name for themselves: the Student Power Team.

A series of four meetings was held to help define the role of the Student Power Team. During the first meeting, the faculty explained to the students that they had been selected for this team because of their work ethic and the positive behavioral influence they had with other students. The students had as their goal for the first meeting to identify the behaviors that posed the greatest impediment to learning and suggest solutions to those problems. The students identified five behaviors that they felt significantly detracted from a positive classroom atmosphere and that fellow students might be able to influence. These problems were talking out, getting out of seats, clowning around, tardiness, and poor attitudes about schoolwork. As possible solutions to these problems, the students suggested that Power Team members serve as hall monitors and role models for other students. More important, however, the students thought that they could help through a peer counseling process.

The second meeting for the Student Power Team focused on how the peer counseling process should be conducted. The institution of a peer helper, peer assistance, or peer counseling program can be a touchy issue in some schools. Therefore, it is critical that appropriate ground rules be established before students begin this process. Most important is that students understand what is appropriate for them to handle and what is not. For the safety of all students, peer advisors must not go further than they are capable of going on any issue. Faculty advisors must help students to have an out when situations arise that might pit one student against another or whenever the information being shared is of a nature that places either student in jeopardy. Students who participate in these types of programs need specific training, and they must understand where the boundaries lie.

During the third meeting, an actual session involving Student Power Team members and other students needing counseling took place. In the sessions, three main points were covered. First, the students were told what positive qualities they had. Next, they were told how the classroom difficulties they had were detracting from the positives that everyone knows they had. Finally, the counseled students were asked for their ideas as to how these classroom problems might be solved. Working together, Student Power Team members and problem students were able to create an environment of care and concern for the learning process. As an outcome of these efforts, the culture of the school moved toward a culture of quality that states, "We are all in this together, and if things are going to get better, we all must do the improving."

The fourth meeting of the Student Power Team focused on what to do with team members who display inappropriate behaviors. In a mature fashion not matched by many adult groups, the students came up with a self-policing policy. A three-step process was created:

1. Peer counseling
2. Suspension from team for 2 weeks
3. Dismissal from team, with replacement by another student

This was an effective leadership step for these students. Many of them were considered to be "special education" students, and this self-policing policy gave them a sense of pride and purpose. Through this process, they fulfilled one of their very important personal needs: the need for the power to control their own lives. Knowing that their teachers were trusting them to help their school was a remarkably empowering experience. The entire process and all procedures were generated from student ideas, and as it can clearly be seen, they are logical, clear, and concise. Given the opportunity and the power, students can and will transform our schools.

Creating Continuity

The middle school students from this rural Illinois community decided that their progress should not stop when they moved on to the high school. To ensure continuity, they created a plan that took student leaders to each of the seven feeder elementary schools. A presentation was made to each of these schools for the purpose of introducing the idea of training selected sixth graders as peer leaders. The middle school student leaders hoped that these students would be their replacements when they moved on to the high school. The teachers at each of the elementary schools agreed that this idea was innovative and had the potential not only to help improve the culture of the middle school but also to improve the climate at the elementary schools. They gave their support and assisted the Student Power Team in setting up the workshops.

One of the middle school staff champions went to the seven elementary schools and administered a student assessment to the sixth-grade students. From this assessment, and through personal interviews, a group of prospective Power Team members was selected. A total of eight students were selected from each elementary school, producing a core of 56 students that would become the nucleus of next year's seventh-grade Power Team. The criteria for selection were the following:

1. A student profile consisting of the qualities of togetherness, enterprise, analytical skills, and motivation
2. Observations regarding commitment to the program, leadership qualities, self-motivation, enthusiasm, and action orientation
3. Balance for the group in terms of gender and cultural diversity

These 56 students were trained in the same manner as were the original Student Power Team members.

The student leadership training challenged the students to confront their own concepts of self and school. They identified their strengths and weaknesses, and they came to realize that where one person was weak, another person was strong. Together, students can complement each other in ways that strengthen the quality culture of the school. The students also learned how to take positive risks and how to put aside the stereotypical roles into which middle school students so easily merge to become authentic, caring human beings. This last aspect also helped identify those students that were not ready for the next step: leadership.

Observations indicated that most of the students met the challenge and were ready to move forward. These leaders began to function together as a supportive team and took responsibility for specific roles. They were immediately given the action assignment of preparing and making a presentation to parents. They were also challenged to find a way to encourage parents to become involved in the project within the next week. The new Student Power Team members readily took on this challenge and produced excellent ideas.

For the future, the vision of the middle school is to involve the elementary, middle, and high school communities in a continuum of quality education. This concept was developed into three specific programs:

1. *Leadership in Action*—Seventh-grade students mentor sixth-grade students
2. *Quality Student Leadership*—Training for sixth-grade students who will join the middle school's Student Power Team
3. *High School Leadership Follow-up*—Ninth-grade students mentor middle school students

The students also created a community forum for the purpose of receiving input from the school's teachers, parents, administrators, and community members. This forum assisted in the development of critical linkages between all stakeholder groups within the school community and promoted the continuation of the student empowerment process.

Project Jumpstart

As was previously stated, there are two approaches that have been used to empower students and transform school cultures. Through the Carnegie Middle School Project, the combination of QSL with the CHAMPS process demonstrated how cocurricular activities can provide an avenue for dramatic cultural change. Project Jumpstart, which is an inner-city elementary project, shows how a more curricular approach can also be effective. This project used the combination of QSL and the CHAMPS process to empower students for a more effective life in the 21st century (see Figure 7.3).

Project Jumpstart is a collaborative intervention strategy initiated by the Illinois State Board of Education. The purpose was to improve student achievement in the lowest achieving schools in Illinois. The specific objective was to increase academic achievement through a strategic approach to the removal of specific barriers to student achievement: inappropriate student behaviors, inadequate

*Communities Honor Achieving, Motivated Positive Students

■ Improve Student Achievement, Test Scores, And The Learning
Environment

■ Better Student Discipline And Attendance

■ School Improvements That Impact Students, Teachers, Parents,
Community

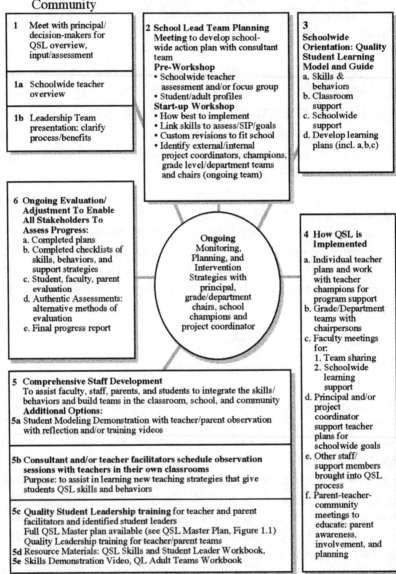

1	Meet with principal/ decision-makers for QSL overview, input/assessment
1a	Schoolwide teacher overview
1b	Leadership Team presentation: clarify process/benefits

2 School Lead Team Planning
Meeting to develop school-wide action plan with consultant team
Pre-Workshop
• Schoolwide teacher assessment and/or focus group
• Student/adult profiles
Start-up Workshop
• How best to implement
• Link skills to assess/SIP/goals
• Custom revisions to fit school
• Identify external/internal project coordinators, champions, grade level/department teams and chairs (ongoing team)

3
Schoolwide Orientation: Quality Student Learning Model and Guide
a. Skills & behaviors
b. Classroom support
c. Schoolwide support
d. Develop learning plans (incl. a,b,c)

6 Ongoing Evaluation/ Adjustment To Enable All Stakeholders To Assess Progress:
a. Completed plans
b. Completed checklists of skills, behaviors, and support strategies
c. Student, faculty, parent evaluation
d. Authentic Assessments: alternative methods of evaluation
e. Final progress report

Ongoing Monitoring, Planning, and Intervention Strategies with principal, grade/department chairs, school champions and project coordinator

4 How QSL is Implemented
a. Individual teacher plans and work with teacher champions for program support
b. Grade/Department teams with chairpersons
c. Faculty meetings for:
 1. Team sharing
 2. Schoolwide learning support
d. Principal and/or project coordinator support teacher plans for schoolwide goals
e. Other staff/ support members brought into QSL process
f. Parent-teacher-community meetings to educate: parent awareness, involvement, and planning

5 Comprehensive Staff Development
To assist faculty, staff, parents, and students to integrate the skills/behaviors and build teams in the classroom, school, and community
Additional Options:
5a Student Modeling Demonstration with teacher/parent observation with reflection and/or training videos

5b Consultant and/or teacher facilitators schedule observation sessions with teachers in their own classrooms
Purpose: to assist in learning new teaching strategies that give students QSL skills and behaviors

5c Quality Student Leadership training for teacher and parent facilitators and identified student leaders
Full QSL Master plan available (see QSL Master Plan, Figure 1.1)
Quality Leadership training for teacher/parent teams
5d Resource Materials: QSL Skills and Student Leader Workbook,
5e Skills Demonstration Video, QL Adult Teams Workbook

Figure 7.3. CHAMPS* Master plan.

attendance, and a nonsupportive life situation outside of school. The effort included a broader vision for the identification of successful intervention strategies that would enable replication and the "scaling up" of this initiative. In addition, it was believed that innovative strategies would ensure that empowered schools would be able to continue their successful efforts once the project had run its course.

Through an invitation by the Illinois State Board of Education, the QSL program (see Figure 7.4) and the CHAMPS support process became integral parts of this unique project. Two inner-city Chicago public elementary schools were the focus of this specific project. The QSL model's purpose is to improve student achievement, the classroom and school learning environment, student behavior and school discipline, and students' lives outside of school. It is intended to produce schoolwide, not just classroom, change. Experienced improvements will have an impact on students, teachers, parents, and the greater community. To accomplish this, students need to learn observable, measurable "school life skills" and make them a permanent part of their behavior. This requires the following steps (see Figure 7.4).

1. The QSL model emphasizes teams and teamwork through school improvement teams. These teams, along with grade and/or department teams, are used to strategize and facilitate student learning of school life skills in the classroom, the school, and the community. Including students in various school improvement meetings and on various teams is integral to the QSL philosophy.

2. (LEARN) As ideas were discussed for making a maximum impact on learning, Illinois State Board of Education staff agreed that eight school life skills should be targeted. These skills addressed the whole child and were identified as being key to developing an effective learning environment for affecting student achievement. The eight school life skills that became a focus of this project were self-directed learning; communication (reading, writing, speaking, and listening); critical thinking; problem solving; creative thinking; goal setting; leadership; and effective relationship building. (IMPROVE) Skill behavior checklists (see example, Figure 7.6) can be used to direct the observation and measurement of student acquisition of the school life skills. The teaching and learning of these skills are much easier when they are spelled out concretely. The checklists empower all stakeholders to work more effectively on the identified skills and behaviors.

1 Use teams and teamwork, such as the School Improvement Team or Grade Level Teams for students to learn school/life skills and behaviors that help improve achievement, the learning environment, student discipline and make them a permanent part of student behavior			
2	**3**	**4**	**5**
L E A R N Teach skills/behaviors that help improve achievement, learning environment and student discipline	Provide the necessary, crucial support for new learning—practice, feedback, coaching, reviewing	Make new skills/behaviors a permanent, integrated part of student behavior	Help improve achievement, learning environment, student discipline and students' lives outside school
I M P R O V E Develop Skill Behavior Checklists for teaching, assessing and improving the learning of School Life Skills

Assess current level of learning or knowledge using the checklists (Pre-assessment)

Track/record current achievement (Pre-tracking) | Develop and use a Classroom Learning Support Checklist to both teach and support learning new skills/behaviors

Use Checklist to assess and improve teaching and support.

Are you making skills/behaviors a part of lesson plans; posting Skill Behavior Checklists; sharing them with parents? | Every month or two assess and improve permanency, integration of new skills, behaviors comparing the results of the last Skill Behavior Checklist assessment with the most recent one

Are there other skills, behaviors, knowledge that are needed? | Assess impact on achievement by comparing pre-tracking with a post-tracking/recording of scores

What has been the improvement? What are the next steps for increasing achievement? What other skills, behaviors, knowledge are required? |

Figure 7.4. Quality Student Learning model.

3. (LEARN) For new learning of skills and behaviors to take place, ongoing support—including practice, feedback, coaching, and reviewing—is vital. This can occur when teachers interface with each other and examine the dimensions of preliminary exposure to the skills and behaviors. Teachers can also practice the skills and behaviors in the classroom using feedback from students to direct improvements in the system. The final link is the home, where parents can also support student learning of the skills and behaviors. (IMPROVE) Classroom learning supports are used to make the skills and behaviors a permanent part of student behavior. Other supports come in the form of lesson planning that incorporates the skills and behaviors and uses activities and assignments that require students to implement what they have learned. By posting the checklists, students have a ready reference constantly available. Schoolwide supports can also be used by announcing a skill or behavior of the day or week and making that behavior a focus in all classes, meetings, and school activities.

4. (LEARN) Make the new skill and/or behavior an integrated part of everyday classroom activities. When students are required to use the skill to perform everyday tasks, students will gain proficiency in the use of that skill. In addition, if students are given activities that extend beyond school that require the use of the skills and behaviors, they will begin to see the relevance of these skills and behaviors to successful living. (IMPROVE) At regular intervals, each teacher completes the QSL Learning Assessment. The feedback will support continuous improvement and assist in assessing permanency of learning the new skills and behaviors.

5. (LEARN/IMPROVE) How have the school results of achievement, learning environment, and discipline been affected by QSL? Schools can use school report cards, surveys, student assessments, anecdotal records, standardized test scores, and questionnaires to gather data. It is important to have established expectations for achievement in each area prior to beginning the project. The baseline data will provide a picture of where the school has started, and each subsequent measurement will tell how far the school has come. With each follow-up measurement, it is necessary for the school to compare progress to expectations and decide whether the methods used are producing the desired outcomes. Considering these assessments, course corrections can be made if they are needed.

The challenge was to bring these skills into every classroom in the school. In too many instances, these types of initiatives are presented in a workshop for teachers and are never implemented with students.

The goal was for teachers, students, and, eventually, parents to be working together to improve the culture for quality learning and, as a consequence, improve student achievement. The process used was the Quality Student Learning program, which is a natural derivative of the QSL model.

As can be seen in the CHAMPS Master Plan (Figure 7.3), this process involved a schoolwide teacher overview (Box 1a) for buy-in and working with a school lead team (Box 1b) to develop a viable, schoolwide action plan. The intervention began during the middle of the spring semester for these two schools. As most educators will attest, this is not the most advantageous time to be introducing new strategies to teachers and their students. Faculty members were focused on existing programs, and there was an underlying attitude of "Here comes the next fad du jour." Sensing this mindset, the consultants had to be excellent listeners and models of the very skills that students would be taught. Through critical and creative thought, the problem of attaining buy-in from a skeptical staff was solved by aligning the program with staff needs. Now, the major push for implementing the program was coming from the staff rather than "outsiders."

In spite of this inauspicious start, both projects moved forward and continued to gain support and acceptance from teachers, who began to see how well their concerns were addressed through the Quality Student Learning process. During the training process, three primary purposes were served.

1. Improvements in the learning environment will increase achievement and raise test scores.
2. Greater focus on responsibility will lead to improved behavior in school and a higher quality of life outside of school.
3. Schoolwide improvements will have an impact on students, teachers, parents, and the community.

To accomplish these purposes, students needed to learn *observable, measurable school life skills and internalize them so as to make them a part of their everyday behavior.* To achieve this, the following action steps were taken:

1. Every adult member modeled all school life skills.
2. Students were taught what each of the school life skills is and how to use them.

3. Skill Behavior Checklists were used to help teachers observe, measure, teach, and improve student application of the eight school life skills.

4. Classroom and schoolwide learning supports were created to help students internalize and incorporate school life skills into their personal behavior systems.

5. Weekly, bimonthly, and monthly classroom and schoolwide learning plans were developed by teacher teams during staff meetings with the assistance of students and parents.

6. Teachers completed the Quality Student Learning Assessment midway through the project and at the completion of the project.

Using these action steps, students learned how to learn and become self-directed learners. They also learned how to get along with one another and help each other build effective, positive relationships. By thinking for themselves and being able to confront and solve the problems they face, students released teachers from the daily struggle of monitoring normal student progress. During this saved time, struggling students could receive remediation for underdeveloped skills. Students also learned how to study as a team and use cooperative learning techniques for the benefit of both the accelerated and challenged students.

Through the use of the Skill Behavior Checklists, teachers were able to define more concretely exactly which behaviors the students were to display. Students will not develop skills unless they can be taught what they need to be able to do. Furthermore, teachers cannot teach skills that they do not understand clearly. Once the teachers started working with the checklists, they began to see the integral part of each behavior, and then they had a better idea as to how they could teach the students to behave. With this clarity of knowledge and understanding, teachers were able to create supports for the process that could be woven into the daily practice of the students. These were developed into schoolwide experiences that were delivered via the weekly, bimonthly, and monthly learning plans. In the end, the teachers were capable of providing detailed feedback as to the quality of student performance in these areas. Time will tell as to whether these efforts have produced a significant improvement in test scores, but day-to-day performance suggests that these students will demonstrate extraordinary gains.

Self-directed Learning	■ Overcomes obstacles to completing a task and completes it ■ Tries to figure out the problem and answer the question before seeking assistance ■ Tries out different solutions and strategies ■ Transfers new learning to real-life situations ■ Asks other students for information ■ Responds to new ideas and information, asking questions, agreeing or disagreeing, etc. ■ Completes the homework/assignments, preparing to learn the next lesson ■ Selects, works on and presents own project
Critical Thinking and Problem Solving	■ Defines the problem ■ Supports opinion/viewpoint with information, facts, or solid reasoning ■ Adds/contributes new ideas and information to help solve the problem ■ Proposes possible solutions ■ Asks questions that assess the soundness of an answer or solution ■ Experiments and decides on a solution ■ Finds out if the chosen solution/answer solved the problem ■ Applies learning from problem-solving to new situations
Teamwork	■ Shares in the work of the group ■ Helps out other students ■ Includes other students in team activities ■ Encourages group members with verbal statements of support ■ Listens and responds to other students' ideas ■ Demonstrates respect, courtesy, and sensitivity to others ■ Acts as a team leader ■ Follows through on team projects and responsibilities
Communication, reading, writing, speaking, listening	■ Listens courteously when others are speaking ■ Writes appropriately for assigned task ■ Organizes, writes and edits assignments ■ Writes and speaks ideas clearly and coherently ■ Listens effectively to instructions and lessons ■ Speaks well in different social situations ■ Reads in order to accomplish specific tasks ■ Engages in productive dialogue with peers and adults

Continued

Figure 7.5. CHAMPS: Quality Student Learning skills.

One of the most important aspects of the Quality Student Learning model was the development of specific, concretely defined dimensions for the eight school life skills. Each dimension became a quality that could be used in a Skill Behavior Checklist. These qualities are shown in Figure 7.5.

Building Effective Relationships	■ Shares appreciation and encouragement with others ■ Practices social courtesies ■ Listens and shares feelings and concerns ■ Exercises conflict prevention and resolution strategies ■ Creates and builds trusting peer relationships ■ Mentors other students and respects cultural diversity ■ Bonds through involvement in authentic projects ■ Establishes student and adult learning partnerships
Goal Setting	■ Identifies specific goals ■ Demonstrates steps in goal setting ■ Sets and meets goals on time ■ Works cooperatively in establishing and meeting goals ■ Adapts goals to changing situations ■ Gives and receives support in accomplishing goals ■ Works in cooperation to define classroom goals ■ Persists and follows through on project goals
Creative Thinking	■ Discovers new viewpoints and solutions to relevant issues ■ Encourages original creative work ■ Writes creatively in expressing oneself ■ Tolerates ambiguity in solving problems ■ Challenges accepted norms and assumptions ■ Integrates principles of various disciplines ■ Allows time for the creative process to unfold ■ Thinks of and uses creative ways of completing a task
Leadership— Individual And Shared	■ Practices different classroom or team roles and responsibilities ■ Cooperates with other students when sharing leadership ■ Accepts and completes individual or group tasks ■ Gives and receives positive and constructive feedback ■ Sets and completes clearly-defined goals ■ Practices tolerance of divergent viewpoints ■ Encourages involvement of all members ■ Shares leadership on classroom, school and community levels

Figure 7.5. (Continued)

Each of the eight school life skills outlined in Figure 7.5 can be used to create a Skill Behavior Checklist. The checklist can then be used to document student growth in each of the eight areas. In this technological age, these qualities can be merged into many different computerized student management systems. This would allow schools to track the development of these skills over the course of a year or from year to year. QSL uses, as a base, the eight previously mentioned skills. Figure 7.6 is an example of one of these—self-directed learning. This skill can be used in several ways:

1. Teachers, parents, and/or students can assess their progress over time using the identified behaviors.
2. Adult and/or student school members can modify the behavior selection by using the QSL skill chart (Figure 7.5).
3. Adult and/or student school members can create other behavior lists specific to identified needs.

Using a checklist of this nature allows a teacher to assess a student's progress continuously, or students can keep track of their own progress. The practicality and simplicity of this system are that it targets observable and measurable student behaviors that not only guide assessment but also create a level of expectancy on the part of participants. One of the problems with many programs is that the expected behaviors are not clearly defined. In the Quality Student Learning materials, students, teachers, parents, and community members work together to develop very specific, clearly defined behaviors that are to be the focus of efforts and growth. One of the key elements of changing student behavior is changing the school culture. When all stakeholders are modeling positive attitudes, beliefs, behaviors, and skills, a climate is established that supports positive cultural change. It is important to realize that culture changes through the actions of community members. Therefore, if what is wanted is a positive cultural change, positive actions must be taken.

Quality Student Learning, Learning Environments, and Student Achievement

At the outset of this project, the question was asked, "How do these school life skills affect student achievement and learning environment?" The elementary teachers worked in grade-level teams and produced lists of reasons why they thought the eight skills would help students improve. Examples from these lists suggest specific beliefs as to why these skills assist in learning and achievement. Because the following lists are taken out of the context of the conducted workshops, they have been modified. Using parentheses clarifies the con-

Self-Directed Learning

Check how often each skill behavior is observed on a scale from (A.) Every day to (E.) Never. The goal is to do each Skill Behavior from (B.) Weekly to (A.) Every day which shows that it has become a permanent part of student behavior

Date _____ Class/Group _____

Skill Behavior	A. Every day	B. Weekly	C. Every 2 weeks	D. Monthly	E. Never
Overcomes obstacles to completing a task and completes it					
Tries to figure out the problem/answer before seeking assistance					
Tries out different solutions and strategies					
Transfers new learning to real-life situations					
Responds to new ideas and information					
Asks other students for information					
Completes homework/assignments preparing to learn the next lesson					
Selects, works on and presents own project					

Figure 7.6. QSL skill behavior checklist.

137

cepts, which have been expanded for readers who did not have the benefit of the discussions taking place during the workshops.

1. Leadership
   - Young people want to be like the leader
   - Leaders bring structure and order, support and guidance
   - You have to be positive to let others know it is OK to make mistakes
   - (Leadership) provides self-esteem, respect, and choice for the children
   - Shared leaderships (creates an environment) in which students can help other students

2. Goal setting
   - (Promotes) time on task
   - Guides and gives direction
   - (Creates an environment that promotes) self-discipline
   - (Creates) opportunities for success
   - (Promotes) improvement of self and/or classroom
   - (Generates) a contractual agreement in either verbal or written form
   - (Focuses efforts on the) acquisition of skills
   - (Promotes) responsibility and accountability

3. Creative thinking
   - Enhances self-esteem
   - Encourages critical thinking
   - (Promotes) looking at other's viewpoint
   - Helps develop communication skills
   - (Provides an opportunity for students to) exert their individuality
   - Develops students' ability to think for themselves
   - Helps students become better writers
   - Helps them develop/recognize analogies
   - Encourages the use of imagination

4. Building effective relationships
   - Students learn better from one another
   - Students need to learn how to care about one another

- Students gain skills they are going to use later in life
- Every class has every type of personality. Children are not surprised when they enter into the real world
- Encouragement and praise (are crucial). Everyone is special. Everyone is important
- Children learn early where praise and knowledge make a positive impact
- Children see the advantage of partnering with the right kind of person in life

From these teacher statements, it can be seen that a direct link between these skills and student achievement was possible. This was an important part of the buy-in process, because those teachers were the ones who had articulated how QSL would help create an improved learning environment. When students learn how to set and take action toward the attainment of goals, they move beyond a world of outward control and into a position of personal control. The key to individual success is taking personal responsibility for one's own growth and development. In too many instances, schools create an environment of dependence rather than independence. As young people acquire a greater understanding of a technologically advanced world, they will remember how they were treated by the purveyors of knowledge. If schools are to have a favorable image in their minds, schools will need to help students learn to become independent yet responsible.

In this process, a major shift must occur. That shift is away from the traditional student-teacher relationship of superior and subordinate. A new relationship that says teachers and students respect each other as people must take precedence. This will lead to an attitude of cooperation and collaboration, which, in turn, will foster problem solving rather than problem blaming. So, as an end product of this training, what did the students have to say about the process? During Project Jumpstart, three skills were given primary focus: teamwork, self-directed learning, and problem solving. Comments from students in Grades 2 through 7 demonstrate how their learning was affected by this training:

Second Grader: Today I learned about teamwork, helping others, solving problems, and doing work together.

Third Grader: I learned to work things out.

Fourth Graders: I learned to share and help people.

I learned that if you help each other and you get the job done, you will learn something.

I learned to work as a team and to follow directions and to focus.

I learned to listen to the teacher and not to disturb other people.

I learned that it is easy to solve problems.

I learned about when you fight, just walk away. And say you are sorry.

Fifth Graders: What I learned . . . is not to give up and [just] do it. I learned how to be a teammate and work together and that I should always be proud of myself. I do not have to be shy all the time.

What I learned today was success.

I learned that trying in life can be good because you never know, you might just do it.

I learned that if you look inside yourself, you will always find someone very good. No matter what size you are you can be anything you want to be.

Sixth Graders: [We came to] understand that we can solve problems.

We have a lot to learn. Something I learned was to talk it out.

Seventh Graders: I learned that if you need help from teachers then ask for it and they will give it to you. If people tell you that you can't be successful, tell them that if you try you can be what you want to be.

I learned that being positive can help you get respect and you can be something in life.

I learned that we can be taught and educated.

These quotations represent a few of the hundreds of students affected by the Quality Student Learning training. Although these statements may not seem like earth-shattering breakthroughs, when they are reviewed in their true context, they take on an added meaning. Remember that the Jumpstart program is being used in inner-city schools in Illinois, where students have been performing well below expected standards. These two inner-city schools using the QSL process have been targeted for intensive assistance in order to turn around the course of education. The first step in this process is to get the members of the school community to believe that they can accomplish the task. From this sampling of quotations from the students, it can be seen that a major shift has occurred.

Once a readiness for education has been established, other good things seem to fall into place. Students of all ages became engaged in the learning process. They were enthused about interacting with the facilitator, and they eagerly volunteered to risk to learn in new situations. Dynamic teaching strategies were modeled and included role playing, presentations, peer support, self-assessment, and reflection on learning. In addition, the process was enhanced by using the following three key teaching support methods (Figure 7.7):

1. QSL
2. Multiple intelligences
3. Authentic assessments

Direct observation suggests that engaged learners are energized by their own success, the opportunity to display originality, the chance to satisfy their natural curiosity, and satisfying relationships. Students who are engaged persist despite challenges and obstacles, and they take visible delight in accomplishing worthwhile goals. Teachers are challenged to create a classroom culture that encourages students to believe that "I can do it. I can be successful."

The classroom learning methods previously mentioned are a vital key in providing this kind of dynamic learning environment. They assist in creating a problem-centered curriculum in which students learn as they create their own solutions to relevant, open-ended problems. Students crave hands-on work across content areas and love to pursue their own areas of interest. It is not necessary to withhold challenges from students. They are not afraid of, nor do they shrink from, hard work. It is essential to keep the literacy target in sight, but it is equally important to realize that there are many forms of literacy. To achieve reading, technological, social, or cultural literacy requires

Multiple Intelligences	QSL Teaching Methods	Authentic Assessment
Verbal	Reframing Empathy	Portfolio Contracts
Logical	Reinforcement Participation Relevancy	Self-assessment I Learned Statements
Visual	Feedback/Correctives Reprimand	Observations Summary Sheets
Body/Kinesthetic	Praise/Acknowledgement Responding	Interviews Participation
Musical	Mutual Respect Relating	Presentations
Intrapersonal	Physical Cues Responsibility Problem-solving skills	Writing/Journaling
Interpersonal	Goal-setting Securing Student Support Of Each Other	Task Assessment
	Humor Recognizing The Gift Of Each Student	Peer Group Evaluation

Note: The three classroom learning methods are not necessarily linked together. Each set of methods stands on their own and can be used in conjunction with the other set of learning methods.

Figure 7.7. QIA classroom learning methods for teachers.

a focus on an engagement in instructionally important tasks. To be literate in trivia is of little or no value to the student or to society as a whole.

Participating students, in their own written evaluations, expressed learnings that affected the human side of education. These so-called soft skills of sharing, helping, cooperating, collaborating, and so on are the very skills that are often cited as most needed in today's world of work. When students make the comment that they learned "sharing and helping people, talking it out, how to treat people, look inside you will find something good," they are saying that they realize how important the quality of our relationships have become. In a world where "quality" has become a buzzword, it is gratifying to see that young people can learn the basic tenets of quality. This type of authentic, caring learning environment facilitates intrinsic motivation and creates a culture that promotes learning and brings out quality behaviors in each and every student.

Teacher Involvement

Initially, teachers were asked to observe the facilitator's student modeling sessions and then to reflect later in the day on what they saw. For subsequent sessions, teachers were invited to become more involved in the process and try some of the new strategies. For example, one teacher came forward and shared with the students that when she was their age, she was shy and faced several challenges. This was a big risk because she was sharing her vulnerability with her students. She quickly found that the students were excited and wanted to support her by giving her ideas that might have helped her be more confident as a student. The entire classroom environment changed, and delight and enthusiasm were seen on the faces of the students. At the same time, the teacher was pleasantly surprised at how easily the culture of the classroom could be transformed from one of struggle to one of cooperation and assistance.

Teachers who were involved in the student modeling sessions were asked to share their experiences and learnings at the schoolwide teacher inservices. This was valuable in that teachers had to form and clearly articulate to their peers their observations and involvement. It also gave the other teachers encouragement that the life skills they knew to be important could also support student achievement and their own professional development.

Teacher Program Evaluations:
Benefit, Value, and What Students Learned

Self-Directed Learning

Students moved away from dependence on teacher-directed instructions to more independent, self-directed learning.

Critical Thinking/Problem Solving

In trying out new solutions, students found that there is not just one answer but several. In addition, they learned that by working together, they could find a best answer to the problems they faced.

Empathy

Students learned to put themselves in someone else's place or situation and experience how that felt. For example, they had to analyze a situation in which a student was being demeaned and then discuss how they would feel and what new coping skills would be used.

Respect, Courtesy, and Sensitivity to Others

Students did acts of kindness using a "Kindness Counts" board. Students posted their names on a card each time they did a kind act. Some students also told about why others deserved to have their names posted. The best outcome occurred when students wanted their peers' names and not just their own on the board.

Teamwork/Cooperative Learning

Teamwork increased learning and brought about a more cohesive atmosphere in the classroom. Students asked each other for information and were very cooperative.

Overall Benefit/Value of Quality Student Learning

- Helps students acquire more skills and behaviors necessary for achievement

- Helps with discipline and how students should conduct themselves outside of the classroom. Improved discipline means student attention or concentration improves, which allows for improved test scores
- Encourages students to do homework
- Promotes cooperation and teamwork between students and teachers
- Helps students grow up with respect, courtesy, and sensitivity to others; learn how to function as respectable citizens of the community; and learn basic skills that normally should be taught at home

Several maxims have grown out of Quality Student Learning/ Project Jumpstart. Each of these supports the finding of numerous research projects that have been conducted over the past decade. Each also has important implications for the future of teaching and learning and the development of learning communities. None of these is profound, yet all are significant.

1. Students of differing abilities and backgrounds are enthused about doing important work. All students benefit from opportunities to explore ideas that have interest and relevance to their lives. All students thrive on the linkage that should exist between what is being taught and how those skills and behaviors will help them achieve their own life goals.

2. Active learning is engaging, whereas passive learning creates distraction. For students to see their work as important, they need to work on real-world problems that link learning to their own existence.

3. All students deserve the opportunity to be reflective and self-monitoring. Teachers can nurture a strong, positive self-image by allowing students to develop an internal locus of control and an awareness of their own strengths and weaknesses.

4. Hard work is not a deterrent to student effort, whereas meaningless, simple busy work is disengaging.

5. Self-esteem is bolstered and motivation enhanced when students accomplish something that was thought to be impossible. Successful completion of tasks that appear to be beyond students' grasp creates more positive self-esteem and motivation than all of the canned programs combined.

6. The challenge for all educators is to move beyond the realm of labels for students and to risk trying new strategies in the classroom. This will produce unexpected results, some of which are successful and some not, but the key to quality learning is not continuous success but continuous improvement. To learn, one must be willing to risk failure.

7. School life skills, such as teamwork and problem solving, go hand in hand with student achievement. They cannot and should not be separated. For those students who have always received "A" grades without learning these skills, what have they really achieved? What merit is there in not being challenged to risk and grow? It is unfortunate that so many of these talented students never learn the skills that will help them be successful in life as well as academics. Education needs to integrate these skills into the academic curriculum to ensure that all students are well-equipped for a society that expects its citizens to make a positive contribution.

Quality Student Learning and Staff Development

Although the Quality Student Learning model has been discussed for individual schools, many school districts are looking to a more cohesive and comprehensive staff development program. Small, independent, shot-in-the-arm programs tend to be cost inefficient and/or often of limited value to the direction and development of the entire school district. An emerging trend is for districts to tie every staff development project directly to the district vision, mission, and goals. In addition, the focus is almost always on improving student achievement.

Functionally, the Quality Student Learning process would be much more effective and could be delivered much more efficiently if it was to be done on a more global basis. A plan was developed for bringing multiple school teams to receive training in order to bring this human technology into their respective schools. The QSL component has been linked to Quality Student Learning to amplify student involvement in the school. Involved students are engaged in the business of school and thus believe in the school's function. This is what will transform the school from an inanimate object into a living, breathing organism.

Figure 7.8 outlines the roles and responsibilities of facilitators (internal or external) in developing the Quality Student Learning

Facilitator		Schools
P H A S E 1	Facilitator presents introduction to CHAMPS Program (Quality Student Learning and Quality Student Leadership)	Principal/representative(s) attend a 2-hr. orientation for awareness/commitment. Identify attendees of Phase 3 start-up workshop school team (grade level/department chairs, etc.), project coordinator and principal
P H A S E 2	Facilitator gives pre-workshop assessment process to individual schools to complete. Each school team brings report to Phase 3 start-up workshop.	School team: bring to Phase 3 start-up a. School organizes existing student needs assessment report. Refer to SIP. b. Student/adult profiles: expected behaviors, attitudes, and skills

P H A S E 3	Facilitator gives one-day start-up process:
	a. Overview of QSLearning and components
	b. How QSLearning is implemented in schools
	c. School Team development: shared vision
	d. Start-up process implementation plan
	  1. Schoolwide learning plan
	  2. Teacher classroom learning plan
	  3. Parent learning plan
	  4. Measurement of progress plan
	  5. Data collection to school project coordinator
	e. Follow-up support options
		QSL School Teams attend to:
		a. Receive Overview of Quality Student Learning process that is aimed at improving student achievement, learning environment, discipline, and student lives outside school.
		b. Create a shared vision for student success.
		c. Develop an implementation plan to bring QSL process back to each school.
		d. After Phase 3 start-up, QSL School Team meets regularly to assess how classroom and schoolwide learning plans are progressing.

Continued

Figure 7.8. Roles and responsibilities of facilitator and schools.

Facilitator	Schools
PHASE 3a	Recommended Option: Facilitator gives individual 2-hour schoolwide orientations to ensure start-up of QSLearning process	(Option) Schoolwide teachers, staff, and other representative stake-holders attend a 2-hour orientation in-service to identify student skill behaviors and develop classroom learning plans that will support the schoolwide learning plan
PHASE 4	Facilitator gives 1-day workshop to support school and grade/department teams for improvement a. Progress reports b. Support schools to develop learning plan based on progress reports c. Teaches classroom learning strategies d. Provides coaching for individual or school cluster teams and grade/department teams e. Mid- and end-of-year evaluations and report on impact of school results/ measurements	QSL School Teams attend to: a. Report out progress b. Review/refine learning plans c. Receive training in classroom strategies d. Develop support plan of school e. After Phase IV: Schools complete mid-and end-of-year evaluator report for impact of school results/ measurements
PHASE 5	Facilitator gives 1-day Quality Student Leadership workshop for school teams of student leaders and staff champion(s)	School team (student leaders, staff champion(s)) attend a 1-day workshop for developing student leadership and supporting the Quality Student Learning process schoolwide

Figure 7.8. (Continued)

process. Many schools are participating in a number of initiatives, with school community members wearing several "hats." This figure gives very clear guidelines for accountability during various phases of the process. This accountability is essential if continuous improvement is to be made. Specifically, during Phase 2 of Figure 7.8, a preworkshop checklist (see Figure 7.9) was used to prepare participants in the start-up workshop (Phase 3). The checklist includes (a) identifying three key school outcomes with measurable indicators; (b) listing social and academic needs data from existing school sources (three desired behaviors, skills, and/or attitudes); (c) identification of current school initiatives where CHAMPS could be naturally integrated; (d) selection of an administrative team; (e) selection of a CHAMPS school leadership team composed of a mix of school stakeholders, including students; (f) consideration of other school/community resources; and (g) identification of two CHAMPS coordinators. This checklist assisted the administrative team in focusing on and preparing for the data that would promote an effective start-up session.

Phase 3, Part c (Schools) of Figure 7.8 is the development of the implementation plan to bring the process back into the school. Note that Figure 7.10 provides a systematic guide for identifying the program (results and performance) and the parallel evaluation (feedback and continuous improvement). Some of the information to be completed in this Program and Evaluation Worksheet will be transferred from Figure 7.9 (preworkshop checklist). Once the school results and indicators are reviewed and inserted on the worksheet (Part 3, Program and Evaluation), proceed to (Part 4, Program) the identification of specific school life skills (see Figure 7.5) that will support the school results. Specific behaviors (Part 4, Evaluation) are then chosen to fit under each skill (see Figure 7.5). A skill/school theme is chosen based upon the desired skills and behaviors. Note that each piece fits to support the other parts of the process in a logical and practical strategy.

Next (Figure 7.10), the support necessary for the success of the program is identified based on input from teachers, administrators, students, and parents (Part 5, Program). After schoolwide program learning supports are identified (Part 5, Evaluation), the goal is to promote permanency of the student behaviors and thus positively influence school results. Strategies for supporting permanent learning of skills and behaviors can be developed during team meetings. Some strategies used at one school were announcing a skill/behavior of the day or week that all classes practice, and using parent-teacher conferences to show parents how to support the learning of skills and behaviors at home.

Administrative Teams' Roles and Responsibilities
(3-member Team)
Preparation for participating in the start-up workshop

❏ 1. Desired school results: (select 1-3 key outcomes) (bring measurable indicators to start-up workshop)

❏ Student achievement	❏ School Unity
❏ Learning environment	❏ Student behavior & discipline
❏ Attendance & punctuality	❏ Parent involvement
❏ Student leadership involvement	❏ Physical environment

❏ Other_____

❏ 2. Pre-workshop Assessment: (bring data to start-up workshop) Identify and bring social academic needs (Use SIP, school report card, surveys, etc.)_____

❏ 3. Identify current (student or adult) initiatives: school programs, curriculum, activities, clubs, plans where CHAMPS could naturally be integrated _____
_____

❏ 4. Principal and/or Administrative Team leadership: provides active leadership.

Names   Positions
_____   _____
_____   _____
_____   _____

❏ 5. Identify attendees for Start-up Workshop: CHAMPS School Leadership Team (maximum 7) comprised of grade level or department chairs, principal, parents, community. (one high/middle school student.) Use existing school management team or organize new team (submit list prior to start-up workshop)

Names   Positions
_____   _____
_____   _____
_____   _____

❏ 5a. Consider other resources in the community/school that can support your on-site school team(s) that can create a true learning community: church, police, Board of Ed, community organizations, etc.
_____

❏ 6. Identify two CHAMPS Co-coordinators: (select from leadership team members). Qualities: Key people who are reliable, follow through on plans, actions and communications. Role: Ongoing communication with external consultant and school team.

Names   Positions
_____   _____
_____   _____
_____   _____

Figure 7.9. CHAMPS preworkshop checklist.

1. Form a School Leadership Team to manage the school program and evaluation development	
Program For Results And Performance	**Evaluation For Feedback And Continuous Improvement**
2. Prepare/build a solid foundation for the CHAMPS school program: **Develop Schoolwide Learning Action Plan**	Develop a Preparation/Foundation Building Checklist: (refer to pre-workshop checklist worksheet) understanding of needs, identify CHAMPS coordinators, etc. Align selected skills (from #4) with current school initiatives below. 1. _____ 2. _____ 3. _____ 4. _____
3. Determine desired school results/ outcomes, such as improved achievement, behavior and discipline, attendance, student leadership, parent involvement, school unity. 1. _____ 2. _____ 3. _____ 4. _____	Develop Results/Outcomes Indicators and Checklist (may choose to work in smaller intra-teams, one result per team). 1. _____ 2. _____ 3. _____ 4. _____
4. Determine skills and behaviors (Refer to your social and academic needs data). School Life Skills (see Figures 7.5) (select skills that will support school results). If working in school result intra-teams, continue with selection of one skill per team. 1. _____ 2. _____ 3. _____ 4. _____ When skills are identified, fill in #2 (Evaluation), fitting skills to current school initiatives.	Develop Action/Behavior Checklist to assess and improve identified skills and behaviors. Pick one key behavior per skill (see Figure 7.5). Note: Grade/department teams will identify additional behaviors that fit their unique classroom situations. 1. _____ 2. _____ 3. _____ 4. _____ Determine the Skill/School Theme from the key desired skills and behaviors for your school that will ultimately impact school results.

Continued

Figure 7.10. CHAMPS program and evaluation worksheet.

Program For Results And Performance	Evaluation For Feedback And Continuous Improvement
5. Determine the necessary, crucial after-program support for the application/use of new skills, behaviors, and knowledge supports. What supports are needed from the following groups? Teachers _____ _____ _____ Administration _____ _____ _____ Students _____ _____ _____ Parents _____ _____ _____	Develop an After-Program Support Checklist and methods to measure progress to assess and improve the necessary after-training support for application, permanency and gaining results. Schoolwide Learning Supports: 1. _____ 2. _____ 3. _____ 4. _____ Additional methods to measure progress: Progress Reports Number of learning plans & results. Number of teachers, parents, students using skills. Number of students' actions demonstrating new skills.
6. Develop the program/learning experience. Do on site with classroom teacher teams: a. Review Chart B overview of process (teachers) b. Review schoolwide skills, behaviors, and skill/school theme identified by your school leadership team c. Grade/department teams select their own behaviors Do on site with students: a. Fill in Chart C student behaviors and actions to demonstrate permanency (students) (see column right) See Resource A for Charts B and C	Develop tests/assessments to assess and improve student learning of required skills and behaviors such as simulated school or life situations, student products, i.e. writing samples, speech, research, project, journal, surveys 1. _____ 2. _____ 3. _____ 4. _____
7. Ensure participant satisfaction with the program	Develop a Participant (teachers, parents, students) Satisfaction Questionnaire
8. CHAMPS Continuous Improvement Process. CHAMPS school coordinators oversee progress report sheets. Distribute to grade/department teams for progress update. School coordinator(s) review with lead team for supporting school teams with appropriate interventions	CHAMPS Continuous Improvement Process Chart: a systematic process that has ongoing progress, monitoring and interventions to ensure continuous quality improvements (fill in names on Chart A). See Resource A a. CHAMPS school coordinators (2) b. School Leadership Team members

Figure 7.10. (Continued)

Once the school leadership team has developed strategies for supporting the learning and internalization of skills and behaviors, the schoolwide learning plan is introduced to grade-level or department teams (Part 6, Program). Reviewing Chart B (Resource A, Figure A.6) will give an overview of the process for a classroom teacher. At this point, the schoolwide skills, behaviors, and skill/school theme are reviewed. With this foundation, the classroom teacher teams now select their own student behaviors and learning supports based on the previous data so that there is consistency. Examples of classroom learning supports are making the school life skills part of lesson plans, homework assignments, classroom discussions concerning the best strategies for learning the skills behaviors, using the skill behaviors to address class problems and issues, and sharing skill behaviors with parents.

Chart C (Figure A.7) would be filled out by students to focus on specific behaviors and actions that they are going to use. Various methods of authentic assessment can be applied to determine the extent of student learning of the required skills and behaviors. Some possibilities are school simulations, journals, presentations, research projects, and/or the creation of model scenarios. In each of these cases, and in others not mentioned, it is essential that the activity has direct relevance to skill behavior use in the learning process.

A participant satisfaction questionnaire can be completed (Figure 7.10, Part 7, Program and Evaluation) by teachers, parents, and students as one method of evaluating progress. CHAMPS Continuous Improvement Process (Part 8, Program and Evaluation) shows the overview of how the school coordinators oversee the process with progress report sheets (Chart A, Figure A.5). These sheets are distributed to grade-level/department teams and returned to school coordinators. The coordinators then review progress with the school leadership team, and appropriate interventions are developed.

It is important to reiterate that each school or community organization is unique, and the CHAMPS process readily adapts to new and diverse situations. Past experience indicates that the worksheets serve as a guide to bring out the creative wisdom of school community members. In this creativity, ownership of the process occurs. Ideas that emerge seem to mold themselves to the school's own situation, environment, and culture.

Phase 5 of Figure 7.8 (Roles and Responsibilities sheet) includes the student leadership training. This student component is vital in that it mobilizes students to demonstrate their ability to make their school a better place. The students know better than anyone which behaviors need to be changed. Once they are allowed to identify positive behaviors and become role models to other students, definite progress occurs in their leadership development. In the Chicago public schools (Region 4) CHAMPS project of 10 schools (a mix of elementary and high schools, including a corrections alternative school), the involvement of dynamic students is integral to the overall success of the program. Each school has identified a core of students, Grades K through 12, who have received training and been involved in the identification of specific skills and behaviors. These students decide on how they will demonstrate those skills and behaviors to fellow students and adults. In many instances, this has involved mentoring or a school improvement project.

In one school, the students went from classroom to classroom to present their ideas through role plays, skits, and question-and-answer sessions. There was a mix of reactions from the student audience, from lively interaction to passive participation. This was part of the student leadership development process—learning how to improve on strategies based on current experiences. To help students process the information they obtained, a series of questions was asked:

1. What did you learn from doing this?
2. What skills did you use?
3. What worked in the classroom presentations?
4. What could be done to improve the presentations?

This reflection was done in small teams and provided a method to integrate the experience and learning into strategies to be used in future presentations.

The student experience not only touched the lives of students, but it also touched the lives of the teachers who were involved. The teachers stated that they gained new insight into their students and student capabilities. The teacher-student relationship was strengthened, as is demonstrated by the following student comments:

"I learned that students and teachers can have a friendship."

"I learned that teachers really do care and that will help me trust them and deal with my problems. I also saw that teachers need help with their problems."

"Teachers are just like us. They are shy, funny, and sometimes scared."

The goal with the highest priority for students was to improve student-teacher relationships. An ad hoc student-teacher steering team was formed to put together ideas for an action plan.

Over and over, these experiences, in real schools with real students and teachers, have shown that the adult-student relationships in a school are vital to creating a quality learning environment. When everyone is working together in a mutual bond of trust and respect, good things happen. This kind of cultural norm does wonders for enhancing learning and creating a feeling of community within schools. The Chicago public schools' Region 4 CHAMPS project culminated in a recognition and celebration (which is in the center part of the Master Plans throughout the book). A core group of 15 students from each of the 10 schools was invited to develop a presentation that demonstrated the positive school life skills and behaviors that were their school's focus (see Figure 7.5 for the eight skills and their respective behaviors). Each school used a unique creative mode to communicate its message (e.g., poetry, improvisation, skits, participatory educational theater, and straight presentation). The opportunity for the students to demonstrate leadership in action as part of a cluster of other school and community members was a highlight of the project and the students' lives.

Education and Corporate Partnerships

Typical business-education partnerships are relationships built on schools asking businesses for financial and/or material support and businesses demanding specific training programs from the schools. In a true alliance of businesses and schools, there is a level of cooperation that says, "How can we help you meet your continuous improvement goals?" Currently, in Sturgis, Michigan, and in inner-city Chicago, these relationships are beginning to yield some extraordinary benefits.

What does this new relationship look like? First of all, both schools and businesses are coming to an agreement as to what students will need to know to be successful in the future. For a while, it looked as if many businesses simply wanted schools to produce workers with the skills that could be generated by a "back to the basics" curriculum.

Today, however, the message has changed. Consider these expectations:

Skills Desired by Fortune 500 Companies
(in order of importance)

1. Teamwork
2. Problem solving
3. Interpersonal skills
4. Oral communication
5. Listening
6. Personal/career development
7. Creative thinking
8. Leadership
9. Goal setting/motivation
10. Writing
11. Organizational effectiveness
12. Computation
13. Reading (From: *Creativity in Action,* Creative Education Foundation, 1990)

Skills for the Workplace of the Future

1. Learning to learn
2. Competence (reading, writing, computation)
3. Communication
4. Adaptability
5. Group effectiveness (*Workplace 2000,* 1992)

Skills Canadian Corporations Want From Prospective Employees

1. People who can communicate, think, and continue to learn throughout their lives
2. People who can demonstrate positive attitudes and behaviors, responsibility, and adaptability
3. People who can work with others (The Conference Board of Canada, 1993)

*Communities Honor Achieving, Motivated, Positive Students

1. Self-Directed Learning   5. Building Effective Relationships
2. Problem Solving   6. Goal-setting
3. Teamwork   7. Creative Thinking
4. Communication   8. Leadership

Figure 7.11. CHAMPS* facilitates top skills development.

As these examples show, the eight Quality Student Learning skills meet businesses' expectations for future employees (Figure 7.11). Schools and businesses must continue to work together so that students will begin to receive the type of information they will need for greater opportunities for a productive future. Together, in cooperation, these alliances will help create higher quality schools. School systems cannot do it alone, nor can governments or businesses. Our destinies are intertwined. Our opportunities are linked, and our outcomes are interdependent. Those who believe that any aspect of our society can remain either independent or dependent are not reading the writing on the walls.

Despite all of the efforts for collaboration between schools, governments, and businesses, a recent U.S. Census Bureau study on hiring, training, and management practices of U.S. businesses found that an alarming gap still remains. The skills that employers say they need are not yet being taught in American schools. This finding further supports the use of approaches like the Quality Student Learning process. Priority must be given to the development of these school life skills for all students in American schools. This is not simply a matter of increasing student achievement; it is a matter of national economic well-being.

One powerful vehicle for supporting youth in their acquisition of the needed skills and preparing them for future career opportunities is the Chicagoland Chamber of Commerce's Youth Motivation Program (YMP). The QSL concepts have been adapted and integrated into an orientation program for volunteer motivational speakers from the business community. This program began as a small experiment in three high schools in Chicago in 1966. Since its small beginnings, it has touched 1.2 million students in more than 50 Chicago public high schools. Today, with the addition of the QSL integrated speaker's orientation program, the YMP has gained support from hundreds of Chicago-area businesses. Approximately 85 business coordinators and more than 1,000 motivational speakers participate in bringing a positive message to the classroom. These messages help to influence the direction taken in the lives of thousands of students every year.

In a much different setting, on a much smaller scale, the Sturgis, Michigan, public schools have also partnered with the Sturgis Area Chamber of Commerce and its Business Education Alliance. In this community, more than 100 local business representatives have been working side by side with classroom teachers. Together, they help students develop the skills that were identified in the previously mentioned reports. As a result of this relationship, cooperation has dramatically improved between the schools and the business community. This has helped students prepare some of the highest quality work to ever be produced by Sturgis students. Evidence of this work can be found in the senior portfolio that each student presents prior to graduation. These senior portfolio presentations involve students showing examples of their quality of work in all academic areas. In addition, they provide evidence of their teamwork and personal management skills to a review panel consisting of business representatives and educators.

Comments from business partners in both of these programs attest to the effectiveness of putting businesses into direct contact with students. Here are a few of the ideas shared:

- "There are people who care, even in today's world. One person CAN make a difference."

- "Bringing Corporate Quality issues to . . . students is a bridge that [QSL has] built."

- "I learned that we should be creative in our interactions with kids."

- "[This training] made me realize, "I" need to keep dreaming my dreams!"

- "[The program] gave me a boost and encouraged me. I am excited and ready to prepare my strategy. I want to change somebody's life."

- "When working with the students, you gain a sense of purpose. You see that these are more than kids, they are our future. I owe it to myself to help them succeed."

- "Before I worked with these kids, I complained a lot about how they never did anything worthwhile. Now I realize that nobody was showing them what businesses needed. At least the businesses weren't. Now we're helping them develop the skills they will need to be better employees and I'm encouraged by what I've seen."

There are definite corporate benefits that result from the participation of businesses. In the future, there will be business-education partnerships that do more than swap resources in every school in America. To accomplish this, however, communities are going to need a vehicle to carry them forward. One vehicle that provides a smooth ride is the Quality Student Leadership/Learning process. Because of the emphasis on personal development, businesses will see:

- A more highly skilled, work-ready labor pool
- Potential employees with an understanding of business etiquette and acceptable norms of behavior and speech
- Fewer dropouts, less violence, less substance abuse, and decreased teenage pregnancy
- Less remedial training for employees
- Lower welfare and prison costs
- Increased community service and corporate responsibility

- Positioning of businesses as key participants in helping youth succeed, which enhances corporate relations with their communities

A Powerful Commitment to Quality:
The Malcolm Baldrige Award for Education

For several years, the Malcolm Baldrige Award has been given to businesses that exemplify quality principles in their daily operations. Recently, a model for using this award mechanism in schools has been piloted. Schools participating in the pilot program had an opportunity to assist program developers in testing the criteria's applicability to education and to make modifications for a wider use in the future. The Sturgis public schools used the criteria, prepared for the education pilot, as part of a state quality initiative in Michigan. The criteria used required participating school districts to evaluate themselves in seven areas:

1. Leadership
2. Information and Analysis
3. Strategic Planning
4. Human Resource Development and Management
5. Process Management
6. Operating Results
7. Customer Focus and Satisfaction

A report document was prepared that explained which strategies were being used in each of these areas and how those strategies affected education in the Sturgis public schools.

Even though no awards were presented in this pilot process, each participating school district received detailed feedback about their operation. As a result of this experience, Sturgis school officials discovered that there were many things that they were doing that contributed significantly to a quality educational experience for their students. Most notable of the success factors was that students were integrally involved in many aspects of school operation. Also significant was the role played by the community in employing quality principles in the process of education. The greatest shortcoming found concerned the need to track customer satisfaction more carefully.

In light of a steady student and community involvement process, the evaluation of the school systems quality program has provided valuable information regarding how to further improve education. The primary focus of all quality systems is continuous improvement. Participating in the Baldrige review process provided specific areas of concern that have since become the focus for future improvements. Each major area of needed improvement has become the focus for a task force. Each task force has been given the opportunity to dream about the possibilities for creating a more ideal school system.

As each task force has taken the Baldrige report and used the information it contains, what has become more and more obvious is that the essential skills taught in the QSL process apply not only to school and classroom settings but also to the living room, city council chamber, churches, and places of business. Perhaps the greatest lesson to be learned is that schools can become excellent sites for education, but they can always get better. With the assistance of an outside agent, schools can gain perspectives that they often miss through internal examination. It is precisely for this reason that schools must undergo an external audit of their financial dealings. The auditors can see things that schools might miss because they are just too close to the situation.

The Malcolm Baldrige Award for Education provides an opportunity for school systems to do both a self-audit of their quality practices and an external audit. This is, indeed, a risk for the school system. It was of great help to the Sturgis public schools to have already been involved with the QSL process, because this established a precedent for external involvement in the assessment of quality. It makes sense to invite an external auditor or consultant to assist the district in assessing its own quality of operation. This audit can be a simple review of adult-student relationships, or it can examine curriculum, instructional practice, stakeholder satisfaction, organizational structure, or many other issues relevant to the operation of a school district. Sturgis, through its participation in the Baldrige process, has gained valuable insight into how it can make an excellent district even better.

A Brighter Future for Schools and
Their Students

The QSL program helps to contribute to the establishment of an educational environment that promotes quality. When schools and businesses collaborate with the help of the QSL process, good things happen. The QSL program can be used to train groups of students, teachers, parents, administrators, business partners, and/or community members. This can be accomplished as separate entities or in a variety of combined groupings. Once trained, teams can carry the banner of quality to the rest of an organization. There are even opportunities for leaders from a school or community to receive trainer training and, as a result, possess the basic skills necessary to train other members of the organization in these quality issues.

Generally, there are four expected outcomes for every QSL workshop (see Figure 7.12, Quality Student Leadership). These outcomes are the following:

1. Identification of areas that need immediate attention as well as those requiring more long-range planning and attention
2. Development of positive relationships between the principal, faculty, students, parents, business partners, and community members
3. Improved student participation in academic, cocurricular, and school/community improvement activities
4. A schoolwide focus on quality issues and the ongoing use of our Quality Leadership processes.

The Quality Student Learning (Figure 7.12, Quality Student Learning) process would be integrated into existing school initiatives and programs. In this way, teachers, counselors, parents, business partners, and community members would receive training to have students in Grades K through 12 using observable, measurable school life skills that will affect achievement and behavior. A comprehensive start-up process would bring school teams together for training. These individuals would return to their respective schools to expand the process. QSLearning and QSLeadership are perfectly aligned to maximize both processes. They are, in turn, aimed at empowering students to be proactive leaders and learners.

Many programs have made a difference in the educational lives of elementary children. The ones that have truly worked, however, are the ones that teach children to take personal responsibility for their own educational growth and development. These programs work because they do not consist of some outside agency "doing something" to the students; the students are doing something to themselves. They also work because the schools that employ the strategies have made a commitment to nurture and enhance those experiences

Figure 7.12. QIA leadership vision.

for children. As the focus shifts from elementary children to "the kids in the middle" and high school students, it can be seen that the same principles apply. If the foundation was laid in the elementary years, the programs can focus on continuing the students' growth and development. If the programs constitute a new experience for the students, they can be just as rewarding and transforming as the experiences for the elementary students.

With the QSL process, each student, teacher, administrator, parent, community member, and/or business partner is asked to make the same commitment: to take personal responsibility for what happens in school. Together, the entire community makes a powerful force for positive growth in students. It is this concept that has created the Sturgis High School vision: "Sturgis High School, Where an Entire Community Helps Every Student Learn." For each entity to operate separately results in such gross weakness that even the slightest change can be traumatic and nearly impossible. It is in the uniting and merging of energies that true, lasting change will take place.

Forging Future Partnerships

In an educational world dominated by quantitative thinking, objectives are important, but they should not drive education. Education
should be driven by a collaborative understanding of the needs of
students, teachers, parents, and the community as a whole. Although
some needs can sometimes be quantified, the more motivating needs
generally are not quantifiable. The magnitude of the work to transform educational paradigms is an enormous undertaking. It is one that
will take a great forging of partnerships in all sectors of school and
community. Quality Improvement Associates (QIA) of Chicago, Illinois, is one organization that has committed its vision and resources
to becoming a champion for children. Figure 7.12 is the leadership vision
that QIA has for the future of America's children. This figure presents
the concept of an international Quality Student Movement in which
adults and students are organized and collaborating in a true community of learners and leaders. The vision of maximizing this specific
leadership process is to create a Quality Leadership Institute and train
networks of adult and student facilitators to bring the idea of student
empowerment and involvement to their schools and communities.

QIA also hopes that many organizations will partner with schools
and communities to assist in the dramatic shift in paradigms that is
needed. There is an ever-increasing opportunity for schools, businesses, governmental groups, and other organizations to explore the
potential for an expanded partnership for the purpose of continuously
improving the quality of education that is offered to all children. The
synergy that results from these partnerships benefits more than the
school. In most instances, the partner receives as many benefits as the
students in the schools. Therefore, it is essential that everyone be open
to all of the possibilities.

In most communities, there are organizations that can work as
partners with schools. In this time when systemic changes are so
greatly needed, the need for these partnerships could not be greater.
In one community, a marvelous partnership between the schools and
a local college has provided an opportunity for both the public schools
and the college to participate in Stephen Covey's Principle-Centered
Leadership training. In another setting, an entire county school system
has partnered with the economic development association to create a
school-to-work program that is truly meeting the needs that students
have voiced as being relevant to their future. And in yet another
community, a local corporation has provided a complete computerized publishing lab and a computer-assisted design lab for student

use. In return, the school has helped the company by developing brochures and design plans with the help of corporate professionals. Students are getting real opportunities to learn real-world skills using real-world machines, and the company has an opportunity to help improve the quality of workers that it might be getting in the future.

Corporations are not the only groups with whom schools can partner. In many communities, service clubs have youth programs to teach students how to be civic minded. The QSL process has been a key to learning these skills in a few of these communities. Its potential for helping other schools develop similar organizations is unlimited. In one school in which QSL has been used, there is a thriving Octagon Club, which is a student branch of Optimist International. In other schools, there are Key Clubs and Beta Clubs. It is not necessary that the school even have a club or organization. Several schools have just adopted a community service focus for their students and have had tremendous success in transforming the lives of both students and community members through the volunteer work the students have done.

One last partnership to mention is a product of a new relationship being built between schools and benevolent foundations. Many schools have active funding to help them create exciting programs for students. The Kellogg Foundation in Battle Creek, Michigan, has provided millions of dollars to schools all across America in their desire to help students become better citizens and develop quality leadership skills. Other foundations have a similar focus, such as the Joyce Foundation, the Mott Foundation, and the Carnegie Foundation, to name just a few. Recently, a combined effort from these foundations and many others has made millions of dollars available to community foundations to set up youth advisory committees (YACs). These committes are made up of youth who use the interest from locally raised money that has been matched by one dollar for every two dollars raised. The match has come from the combined foundations. These YACs use their money to offer grants to local organizations that provide programs and strategies that will enhance the lives of local youth. Some of the most active YACs have been created in communities where the QSL process has been used to help students learn how to lead.

Technology and the Quality Student Leader

In each of the partnerships just discussed, the need for an accurate accounting of data has arisen. The data that must be collected are more detailed and more complex than ever before. Fortunately, technology is providing schools and society with the tools necessary to make sense out of the rapidly increasing volumes of data and information collected on a daily basis. What is done with this information is key to maintaining the positive relationships that have just been forged with these new friends of education. An essential element in this process is the development of a greater respect for everyone involved.

To achieve a new level of respect for all people will require some new approaches to the process of education. Part of this will necessitate the use of new tools for learning and relating. One of the most interesting tools ever developed is the computer, which works remarkably well in the process of acquiring and disseminating information. However, it can also be an albatross. In the process of writing this book, computers have been both.

In many instances, partnering will allow schools to treat students more as individuals rather than as a group. The prospect of individualizing education is frightening to many teachers and administrators because it suggests a record-keeping nightmare. To individually track the progress of each student in his or her academic, social, emotional, and leadership development could create reams of paperwork. This paperwork would probably be filed in student files, which would then be only of limited use to school personnel. With the use of technology, the ability to track and report those same skills, abilities, and behaviors becomes a relatively simple task. In fact, most students can be taught how to keep their own records and update them on a regular basis. With this type of information available, schools will be better able to identify ways that partners can help.

Technology will also help students find new ways to access and use information. In several instances, students who have been trained in the QSL process have contacted one another through Internet accesses. By sharing ideas with other students from different school districts in different states, students have been able to learn about similarities and differences among rural, suburban, and urban school systems. They have also had the opportunity to discover that high school students have the same wants, needs, and desires no matter where their schools are located. In this way, schools have become partners to other schools even though they might be separated by hundreds of miles.

Many schools are wrestling with the technology monster and are not sure exactly how they can make the most efficient and effective use of the technology they have. In addition, many of these schools are not certain as to how they should plan for a technological future. Through the many contacts that QSL facilitators have had, one thing has been made abundantly clear: Students are far less afraid of and concerned about technology than are teachers and administrators. Just as notable is the general lack of student participation on strategic technology planning committees. If schools are really interested in getting the most for their money, does it not make sense to involve the consumer in the process?

From the mouths of students come some wonderful suggestions as to how technology can help improve education. Consider these ideas:

Give every student entering 4th grade a lap-top computer. This costs a lot of money but if we stop buying textbooks and just get the information students need on CD-ROM or something like that, kids will get more excited about learning. Since computers are out of date so fast, they'll probably need to turn in their old ones when they reach high school and get a new one for high school.

Students should be given problems to solve that they should have to use computers to solve. Then they should work in teams to find solutions to the problems. Sometimes there isn't any software that will help students solve the problem so kids will have to learn how to make their own programs. Some kids don't know how to do this but others do. If those that do work with those that don't then eventually everyone will at least know how it is done. Sometimes the kid that knows how to write the program won't understand the science problem or government problem that the team is trying to solve. That's when the team is really important because each person contributes to solving the problem.

We already keep portfolios of our work and skills. It's dumb to be keeping these on paper. We should use computers to keep the information. With the new scanner technology we can take pictures of projects we have completed and store it all on a disk. We could show people our portfolio on a disk. That would save a few trees and when we need to make updates we can just delete the old junk and put in our new stuff.

You ought to put the Quality Student Leadership stuff on CD-ROM. Then kids could get together and create their own leadership development programs and teach themselves. That way they wouldn't have to wait until the school decides to run another workshop or get enough money to hire Mr. Goldman.

- There should be college courses offered on the internet that high school students could take. Instead of driving to the

college to take these classes, the instruction should be on a
homepage that is updated 2 or 3 times a week. Heck, I'd
like to have the opportunity to help a college do this.

As these ideas show, young people have some interesting ideas.
Granted, some of these might be difficult to implement, but shouldn't
educators be listening to students? If students can come up with
creative ideas for using technology, perhaps they can come up with
creative ideas for implementing the concepts. Districts will have to
weigh the situation and mobilize their own students in order to make
progress in the technology area. Schools are in different places with
different resources and will need different plans. By including students in the process, the learning community will gain valuable insights and the students will gain an appreciation for what schools
must deal with to create change. Together, adults and young people
can transform their schools. Is this not the ultimate partnership? A
partnership between teachers and students!

A Final Challenge

Can America achieve Goals 2000? Without a dramatic transformation of American education, it is impossible. It is not realistic to ask a
nation to increase its productivity using the machinery of the early
20th century. Yet American schools are asked to produce the highest
quality math and science students in the world using methods, techniques, strategies, and schools that were primarily designed for the
education needed in 1920. A new vision of education must precede the
development of strategies to achieve Goals 2000. Currently, too many
Americans have a 19th-century attitude about an educational program that needs to prepare students for a 21st-century world.

The QSL Process is one way that communities can transform their
schools. It is too important a job to wait for Washington or your state
capitol to come forward with the means for making the transformation. Each school system and the community that supports that system
must take charge of its own destiny. Massive efforts are needed in
which partners in progress make a personal commitment to the future
of their schools and communities. Companies such as Quality Improvement Associates will assist grassroots efforts to transform
schools who need the help, whereas other communities might take
their own course. Either way, the transformations must take place or
it will just be more of the same. Can we, as a nation, afford that?

Resource A
Charts, Surveys, and Worksheets for Student Empowerment Programs

This section contains a series of figures that is designed to help readers implement student empowerment programs in their own schools.

This is an excellent tool (see Figure A.1) for assessing stages of development for an individual team member as well as the entire team. Each stage builds upon the next stage until a team reaches Stage 4, Mature Closeness. As a team moves through the stages, the members can discuss what attitudes, behaviors, and/or skills will be of assistance in progressing to Stage 4. This stimulates critical thinking, as well as self- and team reflection. The stages are but indicators to increase awareness of where a team is and from where they have progressed. It can also clarify a direction for the future.

This worksheet (see Figure A.2) will assist teams in planning effective, efficient meetings that focus on issues important to the organization. Meetings that are organized and that have specific roles, preparations, and agendas allow for reduced conflict, increased involvement, and desired outcomes. As students share various leadership roles in meetings, they will have a format to assist them in staying on track.

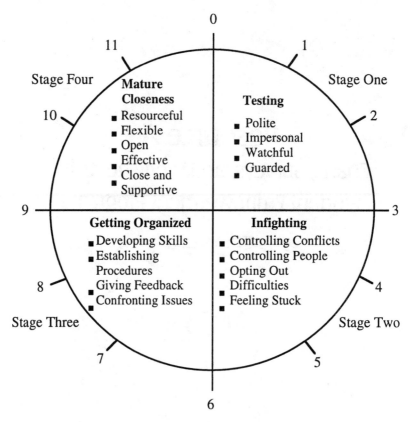

Instructions: Place a mark on the circumference of the wheel to represent the present status of yourself/Team.

Individual Rating:

Team Rating:

Figure A.1. Student Leadership Team assessment wheel.

This survey (see Figure A.3) is intended to facilitate more effective corporate and education partnerships. Businesses can give practical ideas as to what type of support they are willing and able to provide to schools. The time has never been better for businesses to become more active partners in the development of quality education for today's students, their future employees.

This is an out-of-class component (see Figure A.4) that bridges the time between student workshops. After participating in the workshop setting, students will want the opportunity to use the newly acquired

---

1. **MEETING IDENTIFICATION**

   Name of meeting: _____

   Meeting Date: _____

   Meeting times: Starting _____ Ending _____

   Location of the meeting: _____

2. **PURPOSE**: Why was this meeting called? _____

3. **PARTICIPANTS, ROLES** : Who is present at this
   meeting/what meeting roles have been assigned?

   ROLE   PERSON

   Organizer
   (gets people there)   _____

   Coordinator
   (room logistics)   _____

   Scribe (minutes)   _____

   Facilitator (lead meeting)   _____

4. **PREPARATIONS**
   WHAT   WHO
   _____   _____
   _____   _____
   _____   _____

5. **AGENDA**
   ITEM   MEMBER
   _____   _____
   _____   _____
   _____   _____
   _____   _____
   _____   _____

Figure A.2. Meeting management worksheet.

life skills. Students will select challenges from each of the three phases:
self-development, team development, and school and community
leadership. By completing the challenges, students will demonstrate
their ability to integrate leadership skills into their lives and their
community. The pyramid is intended to cover 2 years of middle school
and 4 years of high school. However, it can ultimately work at any
grade level. The high school seniors and graduating eighth graders

6. **ACTION ITEMS:** What will the members of the team do as a result of this meeting?

MEMBER	ACTION	DEADLINE
_____	_____	_____
_____	_____	_____
_____	_____	_____
_____	_____	_____
_____	_____	_____

7. **NEXT MEETING:**

Date of next meeting: _____

Scheduled times: Start _____ End _____

Location of next meeting: _____

PREPARATIONS	MEMBER RESPONSIBLE
_____	_____
_____	_____
_____	_____

8. Facilitator _____
   Organizer _____
   Scribe _____
   Coordinator _____

9. **AGENDA**

ITEM	MEMBER
_____	_____
_____	_____
_____	_____
_____	_____
_____	_____

10. **PROGRESS EVALUATION:** How successful was the group's work on this meeting's agenda?

_____

Figure A.2. (Continued)

can go back to their schools to mentor other students to complete the continuous improvement cycle. Each year, students will work in the three phases of team action challenges (self, team, and school/ community). The challenges each year will increase student involvement, culminating in the high school senior year with developed skills that will assist the students in pursuing gainful employment and/or continued education after high school.

Company Name:_____

Address:_____

Contact Person/Department:_____ Phone #:_____

Alternate Contact:_____ Phone #:_____

Person Referring:_____ Phone #:_____

	Yes	No	N/A
1. Does your company/department have dedicated personnel supporting community programs?			
2. Does your company/department support schools in areas such as: - Mentoring/Training/Coaching			
- Making equipment or supplies available to schools			
3. Would your company/department be available for on site visitations for: - Tours of your facilities			
- Orientation sessions (e.g., job skills or personality traits required)			
Maximum number of students allowed per visit	Number Of Students		
4. Does your company/department have internship opportunities: - Summer job opportunities			
- Apprenticeship			
- Entry-level job training			
5. Would your company/department provide financial support to success-proven programs related to the schools?			
Comments			

Note: N/A stands for non-applicable.

Figure A.3. Corporate resource survey.

This flowchart (see Figure A.5) shows the CHAMPS process that starts with the School Leadership Team and On-Site Coordinators. This team develops the schoolwide learning plan with specific skills and behaviors. These skills and behaviors are then fine-tuned with the grade-level or department teams who chose specific behaviors to be worked on with their students. The coordinators submit a progress report form to the teachers to complete and then return. These data

Figure A.4. CHAMPS: Challenge-Respond Leadership Pyramid.

are used to deliver appropriate interventions for continuous improvement. These behaviors should support current school improvement initiatives rather than add another program. The intended outcome is school community members (students, staff, and administration) working as a team. The team effort should move the team toward the development of measurable knowledge, skills, and behaviors that, in turn, will promote excellence in achievement, learning environment, and self-discipline (refer to Part 8, Figure 7.10).

This flowchart (see Figure A.6) indicates an action team composed of several classroom teachers who choose specific behaviors for their classroom and grade-level/department teams. These behaviors are then made into a skill behavior checklist to monitor progress with students (refer to Parts 6a, 6b, and 6c, Figure 7.10, Program).

This student action worksheet (see Figure A.7) assists students in focusing on the school or skill theme (determined by the school),

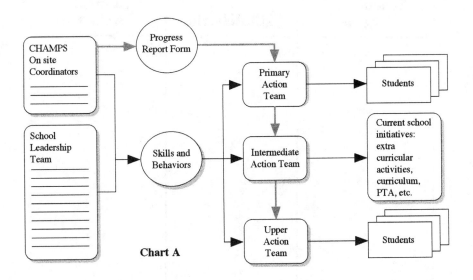

Figure A.5. CHAMPS continuous improvement progress chart.

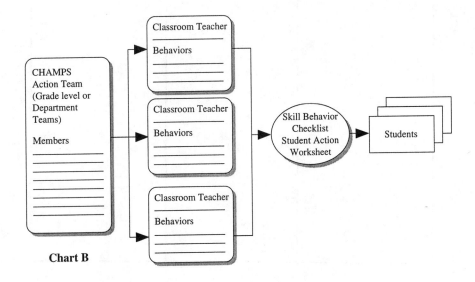

Figure A.6. CHAMPS continuous improvement action team flowchart.

specific skills and behaviors, and student actions. The purpose of this focus is to determine how students will use these skill behaviors to make the behaviors permanent parts of their lives. The demonstration of these skill behaviors can be done in numerous authentic assessment

School/Skill Theme	Skill/Behavior	Student Action

Figure A.7. CHAMPS continuous improvement student action worksheet.

modes (see Part 6, Figure 7.10, [student] Program, and Part 6, Figure 7.10, Evaluation).

This is a template (see Figure A.8) for any school, district, or community organization to complete for supporting their unique

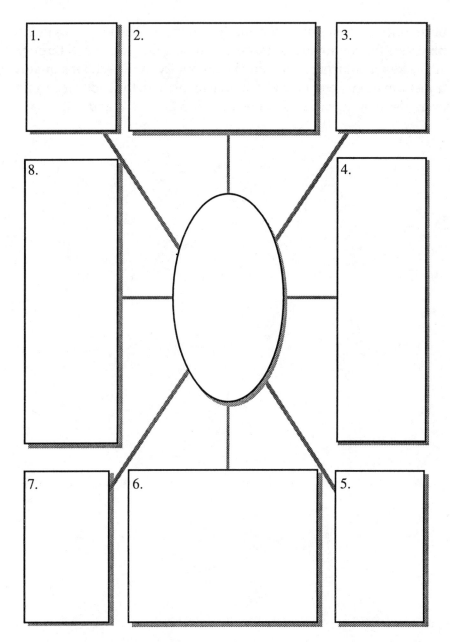

This template may be filled in by individual schools, districts, or
community organizations to align with their unique vision, goals,
and needs. Refer to overall Master Plan (Figure 1.3) and subsequent
Master Plan variations (Figures 4.5, 5.2, 5.3, 7.2, 7.3).

Figure A.8. Master plan for student empowerment.

needs, vision, and goals. Throughout the book, numerous ways have
been demonstrated by which this process can be reformulated based

on an organization's direction and/or priorities. The key focus in this process is the continual intention of involving the students (K through 12) as key members of the school community in the school's quality transformation. Refer to any of the master plans in the book for specific examples of application (Figures 1.3, 4.5, 5.2, 5.3, 7.2, and 7.3).

Resource B
Quality Student Leadership Assessment

INTRAPERSONAL

1. I feel good about myself (self-esteem).

0	1	2	3	4
Do not know	*Strongly disagree*	*Disagree*	*Agree*	*Strongly agree*

Comments _____

_____

2. I am able to deal with personal problems in my life.

0	1	2	3	4
Do not know	*Strongly disagree*	*Disagree*	*Agree*	*Strongly agree*

Comments _____

_____

3. I am a self-confident person.

0	1	2	3	4
Do not know	*Strongly disagree*	*Disagree*	*Agree*	*Strongly agree*

Comments _____

_____

4. I am able to make mistakes and still feel good about myself.

0	1	2	3	4
Do not know	Strongly disagree	Disagree	Agree	Strongly agree

Comments _____

_____

5. I know how to make effective changes in my life.

0	1	2	3	4
Do not know	Strongly disagree	Disagree	Agree	Strongly agree

Comments _____

_____

6. I believe I can be successful in school and in my life.

0	1	2	3	4
Do not know	Strongly disagree	Disagree	Agree	Strongly agree

Comments _____

_____

INTERPERSONAL

7. I feel a part of my school.

0	1	2	3	4
Do not know	Strongly disagree	Disagree	Agree	Strongly agree

Comments _____

_____

_____

8. I have good teamwork skills that I am using in my classroom/school.

0	1	2	3	4
Do not know	Strongly disagree	Disagree	Agree	Strongly agree

Comments _____

_____

_____

9. I have good decision-making skills.

0	1	2	3	4
Do not know	*Strongly disagree*	*Disagree*	*Agree*	*Strongly agree*

Comments _____

_____

_____

10. I have effective communication and presentation skills.

0	1	2	3	4
Do not know	*Strongly disagree*	*Disagree*	*Agree*	*Strongly agree*

Comments _____

_____

_____

11. I feel I have the effective skills to help other students.

0	1	2	3	4
Do not know	*Strongly disagree*	*Disagree*	*Agree*	*Strongly agree*

Comments _____

_____

_____

ACTION

12. I am actively participating and involved in school improvement efforts.

0	1	2	3	4
Do not know	*Strongly disagree*	*Disagree*	*Agree*	*Strongly agree*

Comments _____

_____

13. I have good leadership skills that I am using in my classrooms/school.

0	1	2	3	4
Do not know	*Strongly disagree*	*Disagree*	*Agree*	*Strongly agree*

Comments _____

_____

14. I feel comfortable in working with adults in my classroom/school.

0	1	2	3	4
Do not know	*Strongly disagree*	*Disagree*	*Agree*	*Strongly agree*

Comments _____

_____

_____

15. I know how to make positive changes in my classroom/school.

0	1	2	3	4
Do not know	*Strongly disagree*	*Disagree*	*Agree*	*Strongly agree*

Comments _____

_____

_____

16. I can set goals and put them into action.

0	1	2	3	4
Do not know	*Strongly disagree*	*Disagree*	*Agree*	*Strongly agree*

Comments _____

_____

_____

17. I feel I am able to make a difference in my school and community.

0	1	2	3	4
Do not know	*Strongly disagree*	*Disagree*	*Agree*	*Strongly agree*

Comments _____

_____

_____

Date_____Name/School_____Grade_____

Resource C
Sturgis High School
"Sense of Belonging" Student Survey

Please answer all questions using a 1 to 5 scale.

1 = *never*, 2 = *seldom*, 3 = *usually*, 4 = *frequently*, 5 = *always*.

1. If you come to school in the morning and you are not feeling well, will your teachers show concern for you?

2. If you come to school in the morning and you are not feeling well, will other students show concern for you?

3. If you see new students in the hall, will you help them find their classes and locker?

4. If you see new students in the hall, will you talk to them about school activities and organizations?

5. Do your teachers help new students understand how things are done at this high school?

6. Do teachers help you feel like you are important in this high school?

7. Do your classmates help you feel like you are important in this high school?

8. Do the principal and assistant principal help students feel like they are important in this high school?

9. Have you ever seen the principal or assistant principal help new students find their way around the high school?

10. How often do students get into arguments in school?

11. How often do teachers and students get into arguments in school?

12. Do students show respect to teachers in this school?

13. Do teachers show respect to students in this school?

14. Do students show respect for the principal and assistant principal?

15. Do the principal and assistant principal show respect for the students?

16. If you are upset about something that has happened at school, would you be able to find another student to talk to about the problem?

17. If you are upset about something that has happened at school, would you be able to find a teacher to talk to about the problem?

18. If you are upset about something that has happened at school, would you be able to talk to the principal or assistant principal about the problem?

19. Do you feel welcome when you walk into school each day?

20. Do you try to help other students feel welcome when they walk into school each day?

21. Would you participate in a group that is trying to make SHS a better place for students to learn?

22. In your opinion, how is our school's student discipline program?

23. Do you feel that students receive adequate recognition for their accomplishments?

24. Do you feel that all students are treated equally by teachers?

25. Do you feel that all students are treated equally by other students?

26. Do you feel that all students are treated equally by the principal and assistant principal?

27. How often do students get a chance to participate in leadership activities?

28. How often should students get a chance to participate in leadership activities?

29. How often are students given the opportunity to help one another with academic problems?

30. How often are students given the opportunity to help one another with social problems?

31. Please use the space below to comment on any of the issues covered in the questions above or on any other issue of concern to you.

References

Blankstein, A. M. (1992). Lessons from enlightened corporations. *Educational Leadership, 49*(6), 71-75.

Bonstingl, J. J. (1992). *Schools of quality.* Alexandria, VA: ASCD.

Buschman, L. (1994, March). Less is more. *The Arithmetic Teacher,* pp. 378-380.

Byham, W. C. (1988). *How to improve quality, productivity, and employee satisfaction: Zapp! The lightning of empowerment.* New York: Fawcet Columbine.

Carnegie Council on Adolescent Development. (1989). *Turning points: Preparing American youth for the 21st century* (abr. ed.). New York: Carnegie Corporation of New York.

Costa, A. (1989). *Toward the thinking curriculum: Current cognitive research.* Alexandria, VA: ASCD.

Elias, N. J., & Clabby, J. F. (1988). Teaching social decision making. *Educational Leadership, 45*(6), 52-55.

Fullan, M. (1993). Innovation, reform, and restructuring strategies. In G. Cawelti (Ed.), *Challenges and achievements of American education* (p. 130). Alexandria, VA: ASCD.

Furtwengler, W. J. (1990, April). *Student participation in restructured schools.* Paper presented at the annual meeting of the American Educational Research Association, Boston.

Furtwengler, W. J. (1991, April). *Reducing student misbehavior through student involvement in school restructuring processes.* Paper presented at the annual meeting of the American Educational Research Association, Chicago.

Gardner, H. (1976). *Frames of mind.* New York: Basic Books.

Glasser, W. (1990). *The quality school: Managing students without coercion.* New York: Harper & Row.

Glatthorn, A. A. (1984). *Differentiated supervision.* Alexandria, VA: ASCD.

Goldman, G. (1990). *Quality Student Leadership: A strategy for transforming our schools and communities through direct student involvement.* Chicago: Quality Improvement Associates.

Guilford, J. P. (1967). *The nature of human intelligence.* New York: McGraw-Hill.

Hersey, P., & Blanchard, K. H. (1977). *Management of organizational behavior: Utilizing human resources* (3rd ed.). Englewood Cliffs, NJ: Prentice Hall.

Leithwood, K. A. (1992). The move toward transformational leadership. *Educational Leadership, 49*(5), 8-12.

Levin, B. (1994, June). Putting students at the center: Improving educational productivity. *Phi Delta Kappa.*

Lewis, J. (1986). *Achieving excellence in our schools . . . by taking lessons from America's best run companies.* Westbury, NY: Institute for Advancing Educational Management.

National Commission on Excellence in Education. (1983). *A nation at risk: The imperative for educational reform.* Washington, DC: U.S. Government Printing Office.

Newman, J. B. (1991a). Involving students in school restructuring. *Secondary Education Today, 33*(2), 2-7.

Newman, J. B. (1991b). *Student participation in the NCA/OA process.* Paper presented to the North Central Association, Lansing, MI.

Rinehart, G. (1993). *Quality education.* Milwaukee, WI: Quality Press.

Secretary of Labor's Commission on Achieving Necessary Skills. (1991). *SCANS report.* Washington, DC: U.S. Department of Labor.

Seldes, G. (Ed.). (1985). *The great thoughts.* New York: Ballantine.

Senge, P. M. (1990). *The fifth discipline.* New York: Doubleday.

Sergiovanni, T. J. (1990). Adding value to leadership gets extraordinary results. *Educational Leadership, 47*(8), 23-27.

Sergiovanni, T. J. (1992). Why we should seek substitutes for leadership. *Educational Leadership, 49*(5), 41-45.

Smith, S. C., & Scott, J. J. (1990). *The collaborative school: A work environment for effective instruction.* Eugene, OR: ERIC Clearinghouse on Educational Management.

Spady, W. G. (1988). Organizing for results: The basis of authentic restructuring and reform. *Educational Leadership, 46*(2), 4-8.

Walberg, H. J. (1988). Synthesis of research on time and learning. *Educational Leadership, 45*(6), 76-86.

Schools Referred to in This Book

Chapter 1 Chicago Public Schools: Local School Council Student
   Representatives, Chicago, IL
   Sturgis High School, Sturgis, MI

Chapter 2 Robeson High School, Chicago, IL
   Lakeland Area Education Agency 3, Cylinder, IA

Chapter 3 Iowa Department of Education and Drake University
   Student At-Risk Conference, Des Moines, IA
   Cook County Juvenile Detention Center, Chicago, IL

Chapter 4 Sturgis High School, Sturgis, MI
   Gage Park High School, Chicago, IL

Chapter 5 Sturgis High School, Sturgis, MI
   Benton Community School, Benton, IA
   Amundsen High School, Chicago, IL

Chapter 6 Sturgis High School, Sturgis, MI
   Chicago Vocational High School, Chicago, IL

Chapter 7 Illinois State Board of Education Projects:
   Cahokia Middle School (Carnegie Foundation), Cahokia, IL
   CHAMPS/Jumpstart Project: Henson Elementary School:
   Chicago, IL

Region 4 CHAMPS Project, Chicago Public Schools,
   Chicago, IL:

   Beasley Academic Center
   Cook County Department of Corrections Alternative
      High School
   Fulton Elementary School
   Future Commons High School
   Kenwood High School
   Mays Academy
   McCormick Elementary School
   Murray Language Academy
   Overton Elementary School
   Reavis Math and Science Specialty School
   Chicagoland Chamber of Commerce: Youth Motivation
   Program, Chicago, IL
   Sturgis School District: Malcom Baldridge Award, Sturgis, MI

Empowering Students to Transform Schools Project

Our mission is to be a champion for students, empowering them to transform schools and communities through our leadership technology in creating a true community of learners into the 21st century.

To that end, we desire to be a valued resource to you in your efforts of continuous improvement and lifelong learning. Quality Improvement Associates provides keynote addresses, student and adult workshops and seminars for schools, communities, and business; articles for publications; and newsletters.

We are continually developing strategic alliances with associations, school districts, community organizations, parent organizations, faith-based organizations, and businesses.

Additionally, we have a vision for an international quality student movement. The intention for this movement is to mobilize our youth worldwide and involve them in dynamic projects and synergistic networks for the betterment of humankind. We are interested in collaborating with others in an alliance to support this vision.

For more information regarding any of the above resources and goals, our facilitator certification, or for information about our student and adult leadership workbooks and other materials, please call 773-761-2698 or write to: Quality Improvement Associates, 645 N. Michigan Avenue, Suite 800, Chicago, IL 60611.

From all of us at Quality Improvement Associates, thank you for your commitment to and compassion for our students, and all the children of the world.